This book is dedicated to all those who gave Formula One a red-hot go —and didn't make it. Formula One is motor racing's Mount Everest— and not everyone gets to summit. My old friend Jim Sullivan, arguably Australia's first Driver to Europe scheme recipient (long after New Zealand initiated its program), heads a list of at least twenty Down Under aspirants who gave it everything they had in Europe, but never ultimately put their pedal to F1 metal. They've earned a lifetime of boasting rights.

And, as always, to JJS.

FORMULA ONE

ONE THE AUSTRALIAN AND NEW ZEALAND STORY

JOHN SMAILES

ALLEN&UNWIN
SYDNEY·MELBOURNE·AUCKLAND·LONDON

CONTENTS

FOREWORD

IT'S AN HONOUR TO BE ASKED TO WRITE AN INTRODUCTION
to this book, although as the last Australasian world champion left standing, the choice of those to do it was somewhat limited. After 40 years, I'm impatient to be joined by others on the small podium of Australian world title holders. There were occasions in the last decade when I thought a couple of blokes might make it happen until their boyish enthusiasm got in the way of their steadfast application of talent. Who knows? Maybe in the next five years.

For all the dedication and the self-belief that people throw at it, Formula One remains a game of chance. It's true that you make your own luck, but in F1 the house holds more of the cards than any casino, and the wide-eyed newcomer, pumped up with ambition, is along for the ride—at least until he gathers enough smarts to be able to sense the next move coming (and I don't necessarily mean on the track).

That's what makes this book so intriguing. It's the first time anyone has put together the story of 70 years of Down Under aspiration. With just one exception—Tony Gaze, who did it for the sport—we all started from the same base with the same goal. No one goes F1 racing just to participate. We all want to be world champion. It's an eye-opener to be reminded of how the path to that goal has changed over the years: from Jack Brabham turning up at the Cooper Car Company and building his own car to win his first two world titles, then leaving Cooper to become the only constructor–driver in history to win the world championship; through to me catching the wave of new-style team owners who said they'd build their team around their driver; to the current day, when the multibillion-dollar business of F1 is running its own universities to churn out Bachelors of Formula One, like so many accountancy graduates.

Throughout, the common denominator—the only way to get to the top— is gut-wrenching, single-minded, totally focused determination. Show ponies don't win world titles. Which is why I get frustrated when I see young blokes in the sport—the next generation—wasting their energy on the peripheries of the business. It's as if they're out to win a popularity contest as well as a world title. Formula Three drivers don't need people to carry their helmets. Or am I getting old?

It's only natural that I think of my time in F1 as the golden era. In 1980, tactics and strategies—the hallmarks of contemporary racing—were thin on the ground. We raced wheel-to-wheel without pit stops for 300 kilometres on one set of tyres and on one load of fuel. Power steering didn't exist, and I'd reach down to a five-speed gated gearbox from a perfectly rounded steering wheel that had just one control on it—an engine kill switch. With great relief, I couldn't speak to the pits and they couldn't interfere with me.

Modern-day commentators say F1 has become 'a technical and complex story of competition on so many levels'. They say those of my era were just 'warriors trading blows'. And yet I looked recently at a documentary I'd fronted back in the day, in which I expressed doubt that the 1980s were nearly as much fun as the 1950s and '60s, when times were far simpler. The more things change . . .

I first met author John Smailes at the Monaco GP in 1976 when I was driving for Surtees and on a rickety rung of the ladder that was still a long way from the top. John sensed my frustration, and the opportunities that F1 offered a young journalist, but chose to base himself in Australia where he built a good career and a reputation to match. No doubt he still wonders—what if? At least I was never going to die wondering.

My old man (Stan—winner of the 1959 Australian Grand Prix) was similarly afflicted. He was a red-hot racing driver and, on his day, he could drive Brabham into the weeds. But he had a young son and a business that was going well, so he turned down offers to drive in Europe.

Formula One is for the very few. You don't wish for it. You don't hope for it. You just do it with every fibre of your body. I decided if I turned out not to succeed, I could still look at myself in the mirror and say I'd given it a good go and gathered some stories to live on. This book is full of such stories.

Alan Jones MBE
1980 World F1 Champion

FORMULA ONE FUTURES—THE NEXT GENERATION
Oscar Piastri

AT THE START OF ITS 2021 SEASON JUST 33 DRIVERS HAD won the Formula One world championship. Two, Sir Jack Brabham and Alan Jones, are Australian. One, Denny Hulme, is a New Zealander. By 2021 four Australians had won 42 world championship grands prix (from the 1035 held since the start of Formula One) and that had elevated Australia to a status well above its presumed potential. Of the 39 nationalities that have contested Formula One, Australia is ranked seventh—just one win behind Italy. New Zealand, with twelve grand prix wins shared by two of its drivers, is thirteenth.

In 1947, the just-formed Federation Internationale de l'Automobile (FIA) created Formula One. The World Drivers' Championship began in 1950, the World Constructors' Championship in 1958.

It's tough to win, but young hopefuls, increasingly professional at ever-younger ages, keep coming.

Oscar Piastri's head was suddenly thrust forward. He had been travelling at 277 km/h and in the blink of an eye, he was down to 148: 'It was as if I was going to crush my head on the steering wheel' was how he later described it. His

---

Oscar Piastri's first on-track experience of F1 six-pot carbon brakes, biased to the front, at Sakhir. Drivers use power steering, but power assist brakes are banned so it's their own pedal pressure—up to 150 kilograms—that actuates and modulates braking. The violent move forward under immense braking loads helps the driver to reach that level of intensity.

vision was impaired, his lungs forced against his rib cage, his breath expelled. It was the most violent movement the young racing driver had ever felt inside a car, and for that single moment it threatened his control—and he couldn't wait to feel it again.

At the end of the 2020 international motor-racing season, which had been severely disrupted by the COVID-19 pandemic, Piastri, born in Melbourne, just nineteen years old and the newly crowned FIA Formula Three world champion, had been invited to test a Formula One car for the first time. He was a member of French manufacturer Renault's newly named Alpine Academy, a finishing school for a chosen few racers.

They'd brought him to the Bahrain International Circuit in Sakhir, just at that time of year when the desert heat starts to cool.

Sakhir was a good place to be blooded. It was moderately fast, tenth on the speed table of FIA Grade One tracks. Its lap average over 5.412 kilometres was

Sakhir was ideal for Piastri's first Formula One test. The Renault R.S.18 had scored one of its best ever results at the circuit in 2018 driven by Nico Hülkenberg, whose trace data gave him a direct comparison. It was Piastri's first experience of the kinetic energy recovery system, carbon brakes and an eight-speed semi-automatic gearbox.

more than 211 km/h. Open spaces made it safer for first-timers uneasy with the immense power and immediate reactions of a twitchy, capricious F1 car.

All his racing career—all nine years of it since he'd first driven a go-kart at the age of ten—Piastri had lived intuitively on the edge, instinctively able to balance on the brink of adhesion. As he'd moved up through the junior formulae, he'd learned the art of setting up each car's technology to best respond to his needs.

The Formula One Renault, he anticipated, would be no different—just quicker. If anything, it might even be more controllable. One example: 'It would be the first race car I'd driven with power steering,' he said. Power steering aids driver endurance because grands prix are longer than races for lesser formulae.

Piastri had spent time in Renault's F1 simulator, learning the circuit. The 'sim' replicates as best it can the rise and fall of a circuit and even hints at the physics a driver might experience. But it can't replicate g-force. It might try to trick the driver's mind, to make it look like the scenery around it is rapidly slowing. It might even give a pre-programmed kick in the base of the spine.

But nothing had prepared Piastri for Newton's second law of motion.

A Formula One car is the ultimate prototype. In each new season, Formula One teams set out to reinvent themselves, to be better, faster, stronger, more competitive. Formula One celebrates innovation. Brakes are a prime example.

The human head weighs, give or take, five kilograms. Piastri's safety helmet, purpose-built from lightweight Kevlar, weighed another 1.3 kilograms. At the

The eyes of a racer: Oscar Piastri installed in the Renault R.S.18 before his first ever drive in a Formula One car. His helmet is made of a mixture of Kevlar, titanium, magnesium, aluminium, epoxy resin, carbon fibre, polyethylene and Nomex. His visor is covered in four transparent tear-off strips, each hydrophobically coated for maximum visibility.

end of Sakhir's main straight, braking for the right-hand Schumacher hairpin named for the seven-time world champion, Piastri's Renault R.S.18 generated an incredible 5.2 times the force of gravity in longitudinal deceleration (the Space Shuttle achieved 3g on re-entry into the Earth's atmosphere). In the 1.34 seconds and 83 metres it took to lose 130 km/h of forward motion, his seven neck vertebrae and twenty neck muscles strained to support more than 32 kilograms of Piastri's gravity-enhanced headspace. His head was flying forward in the cockpit at a momentarily undiminished 277 km/h. The helmet–human package hit peak forward deceleration in the first 0.2 seconds, simultaneous with Piastri's left foot exerting 150 kilograms of pressure on the brake pedal.

There were four hard braking points like that on each lap. Add to them 2g's of acceleration and 4–6g's of lateral force in each corner, none of which are supported by a g-suit such as a fighter pilot might wear. Then multiply it by 57 grand prix laps at Sakhir and repeat the process throughout 23 races in the season.

Welcome to Formula One, where even the least performing competitor on the grid is still one of the best drivers in the world.

Piastri was on the trajectory. His record had been exemplary: runner-up in the F4 British Championship at sixteen, winner of the Formula Renault Eurocup at seventeen, and 2020 FIA Formula Three champion at nineteen.

Nothing is ever certain in Formula One but if his progression continued, Piastri could qualify for a Formula One seat before his 21st birthday. If that happened, he would become the 25th driver from Australia and New Zealand to race in the Formula One world championship.

A grand prix victory is the equivalent of winning a Masters tournament in golf or a Grand Slam tournament in tennis. A Formula One world championship is like winning them all in one year. Increasingly, though, it's near impossible even to secure a place on the grid. Statistically, the odds are not in favour of a new entrant from Australasia.

At the beginning of the 2021 season, it had been 40 years since an Australasian had won the world title. Since Alan Jones' victory in 1980, just five Australasians had faced the Formula One world championship starting lights and a determined two, Mark Webber and Daniel Ricciardo, had claimed sixteen grand prix victories between them.

It's just so hard, so competitive, and there are so many elements that have to come together to put a driver in the frame.

At the start of 2021, no Australian had won their home grand prix since it became part of the world championship in 1985.

Formula One is the best motor-racing series in the world. Its rules are designed to reward excellence. Teams are encouraged to interpret them and to imagine ways to bend—but not break—them.

Even when, paradoxically, Formula One seeks to limit performance gains in order to achieve a better competitive balance between its teams, it's really nothing more than an invitation to designers to find a countermeasure. 'Every new regulation brings opportunity once you work out what it means,' says James Allison, chief technical officer of the Mercedes-AMG F1 team that has dominated the last seven years of F1.

It's a fine line. Official acceptance of an innovation is sometimes judged not only by slide rule but by the persuasive argument of the team presenting it to the F1 rule makers. A step beyond what's considered legal lights the fuse. Over

James Allison (right) and seven-time Formula One world champion Sir Lewis Hamilton (knighted in 2021). The bond between driver and engineer is immense. Allison has worked for seven F1 teams and been part of a World Constructors' Championship-winning team twelve times. In 2021 he was promoted to chief technical officer of Mercedes F1.

the seasons, technical breakthroughs, created by geniuses, have been banned amid howls of protest from other teams. Formula One is always at war with itself; it is those battles that have elevated it to the level of prize fighting. Way beyond sport, it's great entertainment on a global level.

Whether it provides the best racing is constantly debated. Other championships—IndyCar, for example—are virtually one-make series that use a common chassis and engine design. Commonality guarantees the closest of competition, but seldom incites controversy. And that's why Formula One remains on top.

The opening grand prix of the first World Drivers' Championship in 1950 pitted nation against nation. It was held on Great Britain's Silverstone circuit in front of King George VI and Queen Elizabeth, and it was a rout for Italy's blood-red

The start of the first grand prix of the first FIA World Drivers' Championship—the British Grand Prix at Silverstone, 13 May 1950. The Alfa Romeo 158s of Giuseppe Farina, Luigi Fagioli and Juan Manuel Fangio lead British driver Reg Parnell. Farina, Fagioli and Parnell finished 1-2-3. The absence of safety separation is by today's standards frightening.

Alfa Romeo team. Britain offered no contemporary competition—it was a slap in the face for the royals and the country. And it spurred on retaliation.

In 1958, when the World Constructors' Championship was inaugurated to recognise the factories as well as the drivers, it was proudly won by Britain's beautifully swoopy Vanwall from Ferrari, while the barking rear-engine Cooper Climaxes snapped at both their heels.

No wonder Jack Brabham wanted to race for the 'mother country'. A whole Formula One industry had grown up in less than a decade. And it was one in which a keen young Australian Grand Prix champion could see a place for himself.

Four years later he was world champion.

Brabham was the guiding light for all Aussies and Kiwis who followed. A man who, as one journalist put it, 'would not use two words when none would do', Brabham let his driving do the talking. He gathered around him a team of mechanics and engineers—most of them Australian—who shared the same philosophy. 'The ambient level of idle chatter in Brabham's workshop,' the journalist said, 'was beneath that of a cloister of Trappist monks.'

'**W**ow. We need the *wow* factor. There needs to be an aura that excites people. When Oscar Piastri walks into a room, people need to stop and know he's there.'

Mia Sharizman, head of Renault's Alpine Academy, had been Piastri's mentor for almost eighteen months since he won the 2019 Formula Renault Eurocup and qualified to join the company's driver development program.

'He's quick, he's calm, intelligent, with a maturity beyond his age. [But] he's cool, chilled,' Sharizman said of Piastri. 'A racing team needs to be excited about a driver. I say to him: "Go and learn the name of someone on the shop floor—just one. The word will soon spread and they'll get behind you."'

In Malaysia, sixteen years earlier, Sharizman had been running the Asian end of the Formula BMW junior series—a feeder program that unearthed serious talent including world champions Sebastian Vettel and Nico Rosberg—when a young Aussie turned up.

'He had curly hair and goofy teeth and even when he flipped his car, he was smiling all the time.' It was Sharizman's first encounter with Daniel Ricciardo and he holds the Western Australian up as a model of the 'wow factor'. 'People see you're here to win the championship and that helps you go further.'

In 2020, a change came over Piastri. He became 'Mr Twitter'. 'No one knew who he was and then he started to tweet. He was funny, witty, and became the Twitter voice of Formula Three.' In a mature sport, run by senior people, social media had emerged as the new way of talking and Piastri had nailed it.

Like Brabham, he was also doing his talking on the track: 'There was a moment at Monza [F1's fastest track] when he went three abreast and all their wheels interlocked, and Oscar wouldn't relent. That sort of thing sticks in people's mind,' Sharizman recounted. Above any concerns he had about his young driver's persona,

Opposite: Renault's class of 2020: Alpine Academy director Mia Sharizman (far left); Daniel Ricciardo (fifth from left); new recruit Oscar Piastri (third from right); and Alain Prost, 'the Professor', Renault hero and four-time Formula One world champion (far right).

Above: Wheel to wheel, three abreast, over the rise at the Red Bull Ring, Austria, in round 2 of the 2020 FIA Formula 3 Championship. Left to right: Oscar Piastri (#1), Oliver Caldwell (#12) and Frederik Vesti (#2). Vesti won the race; Piastri won the championship.

Sharizman recognised that skill and speed were the predominant characteristics he sought, and Piastri had both.

Nicole Piastri knew her life had changed forever just after midnight on a chilly night in 2014. Her thirteen-year-old son Oscar was racing in the junior division of the IAME International World Karting Championship in Le Mans; she'd

It all started here: nine-year-old Oscar Piastri and his dad Chris, category winners in the 2010 National On Road Remote Control Car Championship at Bendigo's Strathdale Park. Oscar won the Super Stock A-class; Chris, the Stock A-class. The following year, Oscar graduated to karts.

tucked Oscar's three younger sisters into bed and was live-streaming his race in her living room in Melbourne's bayside suburb of Brighton. 'I'd made a deal with Oscar and Chris [her husband] that if he didn't do well, he'd return to his studies in Australia.' Oscar was on an academic scholarship at private school Haileybury.

Oscar started his race from 21st position. 'I was thinking, "In about half an hour my life is going to get a lot easier." But then he started to move up and it looked like everyone else was in slo-mo, and the commentator kept calling his name and then he got to third, and his name disappeared from the timing. And then the commentator came back on and announced him on the podium. I cried out, "No!" I didn't want him moving overseas. He doesn't have to be a Formula One driver. He's just having fun.'

Oscar had been an Australian remote-control car-racing champion at age nine. He beat a much older seventeen-year-old ('At nine, your reflexes are pretty good,' he grinned). It helped that his father, Chris, is an electronics genius. His business, which is based in Chicago but runs from wherever he is in the world, is called HP Tuners and it grew out of Chris's passion for making big American iron go fast.

Remote-control cars led to karts. Australian success led to Le Mans. At thirteen, Oscar, with Chris at his side, became a FIFO (fly-in fly-out) racer, and when he was fourteen they moved to the UK to be close to the action, leaving Nicole and the girls behind. It wasn't a great solution, and Chris and Nicole couldn't sustain it. Oscar entered boarding school in the UK—also called Haileybury—to maintain his education, and conducted his racing career from the dorm while Chris returned to Australia.

In 2020, remarkably, Oscar won the FIA Formula 3 Championship, and passed his A Levels. 'It was a good decision to stay in school,' Oscar offered, with a maturity that is frankly astounding. 'I know how quickly things can change, and besides, school gave me a focus outside of racing.'

Two world champions in 2020: Oscar Piastri (left), the F3 champion, and Mick Schumacher, son of Michael, F2 champion, both disguised by masks worn for COVID-19. Mick moved to Formula One in 2021 with the Haas-Ferrari team; Oscar was promoted to Mick's place in the Prema Formula Two team.

Chris concurred. 'A lot of the kids you see in the racing paddock haven't been to school. If it doesn't work out, what have they got?'

For a motor-racing novice, Chris had managed his son's progress astutely. Armed with a large enough budget, he'd chosen the right teams for his son. It's a predatory pond, and one wrong decision can sink a career. 'I've been lucky,' Oscar acknowledged.

Chris was a little coy to reveal precisely the scope of his investment . . . perhaps he honestly didn't care to know. But 'a lower-ranking Formula Three drive is around €700,000 [A$1.1 million] for the season, a top team €1 million [A$1.5 million],' Chris said. Oscar had secured a top team. 'For a Formula Two drive you can double those numbers. That's for the team, not counting living and travel expenses.'

When Oscar joined the Alpine Academy, some—though not all—of the pressure was relieved.

A different kind of mask: Oscar Piastri undertakes low-oxygen training with noted exercise physiologist Simon Sostaric. The sports scientist worked with Mark Webber to develop F1-specific strategies; Piastri is the first driver Sostaric has been associated with from the junior categories. In preparation for Piastri's entry into the highly demanding F2 category, he put on four kilograms of muscle in three months.

'It's a partnership,' Mia Sharizman said. 'We'll pay between 25 and 50 per cent of the cost of a driver's development. The family [or backers—a government, for example] pay the rest.'

Alpine's policy is to embrace the parents rather than exclude them. Parental care is even more important than looking after the young driver's manager. 'You can always change a manager, but a kid will listen to their parent first, then us,' Sharizman observed.

Alpine 'met' Oscar late in his development. They wrote him a four-year plan—progressing through Formula Three, then Formula Two, right up to Formula One. If he goes all the way, he'll be the first graduate of Alpine's program to achieve the goal within the team.

The second half of that four-year plan is critical. Every facet of car control, even of the driver's physiology, needs to adapt to each next phase. Some will make it; others will not. And Oscar is not being developed in isolation. At least another two aspirants are on his level.

Oscar Piastri was sixteen when he was runner-up in the 2017 F4 British Championship, with six pole positions and six wins. Four seasons on he had progressed through three other categories, winning two of them, and was knocking on the door of Formula One. The vagaries of motor racing are immense. In 2021, the driver who had beaten Piastri back in 2017 was still in F4.

'We cannot hedge everything into one basket. The more the level of competition, the higher we can set the bar,' Sharizman said. He knows there are some he will have to let down: 'Before you hire, you have to think about how you're going to fire.' It is simply the reality of Formula One life.

Oscar accepted that, but he and Chris had made the decision to willingly enter the shelter of the Alpine tent rather than go it alone. 'There's no way I can drop $100 million on a Formula One race team to have Oscar join them. There are no eight- or nine-figure sums available,' Chris said. Alpine understood this. 'Even a well-to-do family can't afford Formula One,' said Sharizman. 'Just a Formula One test could cost as much as running an entire championship series in Formula Four.'

In early February 2021, in the midst of the pandemic that had halted all but the most pressingly urgent international air travel, Oscar Piastri found a way to fly out of Melbourne bound for an Alpine Academy training session in Tenerife in the Canary Islands. His teammates were going to be there and there was no way he was going to be left out—or left behind.

2

IN THE BEGINNING— GRAND ÉPREUVE
Arthur Waite
Bernard Rubin
Joan Richmond

ORIGINALLY, THE FRENCH HAD CALLED GRAND PRIX racing 'grand épreuve' ('grand test'), and as early as 1906 it defined the very top end of competition, providing a platform for the world's fledgling car industry to showcase and prove its products.

Whole nationalities claimed the Grand Épreuve as their country's premier event. Their cars were assigned national colours: blue for France, red for Italy, green for Britain. They raced for sales success and national honour. Then the Germans arrived—and they raced for propaganda. After initially producing white cars, Mercedes left off the paint in 1934 to save weight, exposing the bare, shining metal, so the German cars became the 'Silver Arrows'.

By the mid-1930s, there were no fewer than eighteen grands prix in operation, including Australia's.

Three Australians sought the adventure of European racing in the decade before World War II.

Australia's first female international race winner, Joan Richmond, with just some of the trophies that marked her incredible career. Some have been lost, but a substantial collection exists in the National Museum of Australia.

Above: The first ever grand prix, and the first ever winner—Hungarian driver Ferenc Szisz, for Renault—leads on the long straight of Le Mans at the French Grand Prix, 26–27 June 1906. Chasing him is American driver Elliott Shepard (Hotchkiss), who retired with wheel failure on the seventh of twelve 103.18-kilometre laps raced over two days.

Left: Germany's Silver Arrows (Mercedes-Benz and Auto Union) dominated the 1937 Donington Grand Prix. Bernd Rosemeyer, Manfred von Brauchitsch and Rudolf Caracciola literally flew to the first three positions—a massive show of pre–World War II strength.

ARTHUR WAITE

Captain Arthur Waite MC, veteran of the Gallipoli campaign in World War 1 and international racing driver, simply couldn't believe his eyes. There he was, driving to plan in the very first Australian Grand Prix in 1928, guiding his tiny Austin 7 to what he hoped would be a podium finish against much quicker machinery, when he passed the race favourite Arthur Terdich.

Terdich wasn't at the wheel of his Bugatti T40—the fastest car in the field—but perched precariously on the back of another car, clinging to three jerry cans of fuel. With just two laps to go and with a commanding lead on the Phillip Island circuit south of Melbourne, the last isthmus of mainland before Antarctica, Terdich's car had spluttered and stopped. He'd quickly hailed down another competitor, hitched a ride to the pits and grabbed the fuel.

But when he arrived at the spot he'd left the Bugatti, it wasn't there. Terdich's riding mechanic had fixed a fuel feed problem, fired up the Bug and torn off to the pits in search of his driver. Terdich had to do an extra lap to find him, then powered on to claim fourth outright. By the time he crossed the line Arthur Waite, resplendent in white racing overalls, Herbie Johnson–type helmet and metal-rimmed aviator goggles, had already been chaired to the victory dais.

Waite—son-in-law of Sir Herbert Austin, founder of the Austin Motor Company—had already won in Europe, in his division of the International Grand Prix for Light Cars at Monza in 1923, becoming the first Australian to win a grand prix on foreign soil. And now, on 26 March 1928, he had just become the first Australian to win a grand prix in his home country.

The 'Baby Austin' Waite used for both grand prix victories had turned around the fortunes of his father-in-law's company. The 750cc Austin had been built to a budget and, more importantly, to a strict manufacturing discipline. At launch, its initial price in Britain had been capped at £225 [A$413], and Austin reduced that each year as volumes rose, making it even more accessible to the average family. Waite was part of its success. He'd been a development engineer on the project and its chief test driver.

Born in Adelaide in 1894 and trained as an engineer, he'd shipped out at the start of World War 1, fought his way ashore at Gallipoli on 25 April 1915 and been severely wounded in France. In hospital, he met nurse Irene Austin. Irene's brother Vernon, the only son of Sir Herbert, had been killed in action. When Arthur and Irene married in October 1918, Arthur was welcomed into the family as their new son.

Above: Australia's first grand prix winner. Captain Arthur Waite (Austin 7) crosses the finish line at Phillip Island in 1928 to take what many called the luckiest of victories. More than 90 years later a reconstruction of the boat-like bodywork of Waite's Austin 7, reunited with the car's actual supercharged drivetrain, is revered by enthusiasts. Waite's Austin 7 featured on a commemorative 45-cent Australia Post stamp issued in 2014 to mark the centenary of motor racing in Australia.

Right: Arthur Waite is chaired to victory after winning the 1928 Australian Grand Prix. Waite and mechanic Guy Barringer had driven their tiny Austin only once before the race—in a Melbourne lane, where they had confirmed a top speed of 144 km/h.

At Monza, Italy, in 1923, Arthur Waite (far left) with riding mechanic Alf Depper (second from left) won the International Grand Prix for Light Cars. The Austin team, proudly overseen by Sir Herbert Austin (far right), was a model of professional presentation.

The Great War had broken Herbert Austin's heart and very nearly his company. The knighthood he was awarded for turning his factory over to the war effort did not alleviate the financial stress. Austin appointed receivers in 1921, but they let him build the Baby Austin and it took off.

Arthur Waite spearheaded a 'win on Sunday, sell on Monday' promotional blitz. He set class speed records at the banked Brooklands circuit outside London and, in early 1923, drove a race-prepared Austin 7 all the way to Monza in northern Italy to contest the International Grand Prix for Light Cars.

He overwhelmed the 750cc category, blowing away the locally made Anzani. (Alessandro Anzani's engine had powered Louis Blériot on the first flight across the English Channel in 1909.) Beating the Anzani boosted Austin's reputation.

In 1927, Sir Herbert sent Irene and Arthur to Australia to help the local Austin distributor 'double sales'. It was part of his succession plan, to round out their experience. Waite asked that his grand prix car be shipped down to him for the 1928 Australian Grand Prix. When he opened the crate, he didn't find his red-hot race car (it had been sold), but a sports prototype. Still, it would be the only supercharged car in the grand prix. It had a four-speed gearbox—the extra forward gear replaced reverse in the tiny casing, and chassis, suspension and brakes had all been 'tuned'. It was ideal for the conditions Phillip Island threw up.

The Waites returned to the UK in 1929, but clear succession was no longer an option. A board had taken control of the company. Waite became director in charge of sales, service and promotions, and retired from active competition after a crash in the 1930 Ards TT in Northern Ireland. Arthur Waite died in 1991, aged 96. He and Irene did not leave an heir.

BERNARD RUBIN AND THE BENTLEY BOYS

In 1929, Bernard Rubin, born in Melbourne, claimed eighth place in the first Irish Grand Prix, a 488-kilometre dash around Dublin's Phoenix Park. After Arthur Waite, he'd become only the second Australian to race in a European grand prix. He would go on to be a team owner in the most controversial GP of the pre-war era.

Rubin, heir to a fabulous Kimberley pearl fortune, shared digs at 50 Grosvenor Square in London's exclusive Mayfair with Woolf Barnato, heir to a fabulous South African diamond and gold fortune. Their lifestyles were not understated.

Bernard Rubin, son of a Lithuanian immigrant who made a fortune pearl trading in Western Australia's Kimberley region, was educated in Broome and moved to the United Kingdom at age fifteen. He maintained ties with Australia through ownership of vast cattle stations, including the 19,700-hectare Northampton Downs station in Queensland. His inheritance funded his motor racing.

In 1926, aged 31, Barnato used a tiny portion of his wealth to bail Bentley Motors out of impending financial doom. He left W.O. Bentley in charge. Barnato was in it for the sport. He gathered around him a group of wealthy young sportsmen who became known collectively as the Bentley Boys. There were so many Bentleys parked in Grosvenor Square that taxi drivers knew it as Bentley Corner.

In 1919, Bentley had been launched with great optimism at the British Motor Show, and Barnato had quickly become its star driver, even setting a new three-litre 24-hour record of 152 km/h on the newly opened, steeply banked 2.5-kilometre Autodrome de Montlhéry south of Paris. And then he bought the company.

Bernard Rubin caught the bug. In 1928, he and Barnato won the Le Mans 24 Hour race in their 4.5-litre Bentley. Rubin had been racing for less than six months, but far from implying that the more experienced Barnato carried the result, it was Rubin's efforts in the middle stages, dicing wheel to wheel with the American Stutz team, that were hailed as the pivot point. A year later, he reinforced that with his eighth place in the Irish Grand Prix.

Woolf Barnato (left) and Bernard Rubin co-drove the 4.5-litre Bentley that won the Le Mans 24 Hour race in 1928. Bentley won four Le Mans races in succession from 1927.

A month on, at the International Tourist Trophy, a grand prix in all but name, Rubin debuted the 4.5-litre 'Blower' Bentley—the car commissioned by another Bentley Boy, Sir Henry 'Tim' Birkin, against W.O. Bentley's advice—and on lap one he rolled it, aggravating injuries he'd received in World War 1. It was time to reassess. Rather than be a driver, he reasoned, he would become a team owner, a patron, and Birkin, who'd lost most of his family's fortune on the 'Blower' project, would be the beneficiary.

Le Mans, 1928. In the early morning, Bernard Rubin increased the Bentley's lead on Robert Bloch's Stutz Blackhawk then handed back to Barnato, who nursed the car home with a leaking radiator to finish one lap ahead.

The pair barnstormed Europe, no longer in Bentleys but on Alfa Romeo and K3MG. In 1933, Rubin acquired a Maserati 8C 3000 and entered the Tripoli Grand Prix—the most controversial grand prix ever held. 'The race was rigged,' Mercedes' team manager Alfred Neubauer thundered in his autobiography. And he was right.

The Italian government had determined to run a national lottery on the outcome of the Tripoli Grand Prix, a massive fundraiser for the fascist state signed off by Benito Mussolini. The lottery raised fifteen million lire at twelve lire a ticket. Thirty ticket holders, drawn at random, would be matched with the 30 entrants—three million lire for first, two million for second, one million for third. The massive surplus would go to the government.

The favourites decided they wanted a share. In a clandestine huddle, the top three—Achille Varzi (Bugatti), Tazio Nuvolari (Alfa Romeo) and Mario Borzacchini (Alfa Romeo)—met with their corresponding ticket holders and created a prize pool from which they would all draw evenly, lottery winners and drivers alike. First, second and third would pay the same; the outcome no longer mattered. Except: what if an outsider got up? They offered Tim Birkin, the stiff-upper-lipped Englishman in Rubin's car, somewhere between 70,000 and 100,000 lire not to interfere.

Birkin stormed away from the front-row start and led at the end of the first lap, but dropped back. Borzacchini hit an oil drum mid-race and retired, leaving Varzi and Nuvolari to fight it

The 1933 Tripoli Grand Prix is infamous in motor racing for its alleged race fixing by some of the biggest names in the sport.

out. They finished just 0.2 seconds apart—surely not contrived—and Birkin came third, 1 minute 31 seconds behind. Officials were onto the scam, but to disqualify Europe's finest drivers would have been a black mark on the sport so they were merely cautioned and the results stood.

As team patron, it was Bernard Rubin's greatest triumph, but it was also to be Tim Birkin's last race. In the pits, refuelling at half-distance, he reached out to accept a cigarette and burned his arm on the exhaust. The wound became infected and, a month later, he died. Bernard Rubin died in England in 1936, aged just 39, of tuberculosis. At his instructions, his remains were returned to Melbourne where he was interred alongside his father.

JOAN RICHMOND

In 1931, Joan Richmond, daughter of one of Australia's pioneer wool growers, became the first woman to drive in the Australian Grand Prix. In a Brooklands Riley, with riding mechanic Mollie Shaw alongside, she came fifth in her country's premier motor race. It was the start of an international career.

Within a year, Richmond teamed with Elsie Wisdom, Britain's leading female racing driver of the era, and won the Brooklands 1000 Miles Race: not just first in their class, nor the first female drivers home, but outright. They outdistanced and outlasted some of the biggest names, and brands, in the sport. 'Elsie and I were the first women to win a major race open to all comers. The press regarded our win very favourably,' she understated.

In a seven-year European campaign, she competed in the Monte Carlo Rally, the Le Mans 24 Hour, national championship hill climbs, Tourist Trophy races and land speed events—everything except a grand prix. That ambition was thwarted by World War II.

Richmond started motor racing because her gender barred her from being a jockey. 'I was furious and devastated. I couldn't see what being a man or a woman had to do with being able to ride a horse,' she told her biographer David Price. 'But I could race a car.' The Richmonds developed one of the country's most successful merino studs, Haddon Rig, then sold it to another pioneering family, the Falkiners, in 1916. It had been a forced sale, brought on by illness. By the time Richmond was 21, both her grandfather and father had died, and she was left with what she called 'a small legacy'. Her family's chauffeur taught her to drive.

Joan Richmond (left) and Mollie Shaw claimed fifth outright in the 1931 Australian Grand Prix at Phillip Island. Their Brooklands Riley finished on the same lap as winner Carl Junker's Bugatti T39. They were sixth on handicap.

The 1931 Australian Grand Prix at Phillip Island was the first to be run as a handicap. The supercharged Bugattis of Arthur Terdich and Hope Bartlett were off scratch, which meant they started last and had to hunt down slower cars. Richmond and Shaw attracted publicity because of their gender, but no favour. They were off 22 minutes ahead of the scratch starters, in the middle of the pack in their class. It was Richmond's 26th birthday.

'The total race distance was to be 206 miles [331 kilometres], further than I had ever raced before,' she told her biographer. 'There was very little accommodation on the island, most of us set up our tents and camped alongside the racetrack. The roads were unsealed dirt and although the oil companies were in the habit of donating surplus used oil to sprinkle on the track, the dust was vile.'

Nineteen cars entered. Six finished. Melbourne's Carl Junker won in a Bugatti T39 at an average speed of 112.42 km/h. Richmond and Shaw were consistent throughout. A measure of a good driver is how they maintain their pace. Richmond's average was 91.84 km/h, and that was faster than Arthur Waite's 90.5 km/h when he'd won the inaugural Australian Grand Prix just four years before.

Richmond arrived in the UK six months later—not conventionally but overland. Less than four years after Australian adventurer Francis Birtles accomplished the first ever overland automotive crossing from Great Britain to Australia, a death-defying horror journey, Joan did it in the reverse direction. The Riley car company mounted a three-car team with four women, a token male and a matronly chaperone. In fairness, they did not completely follow Birtles' harsh overland route. Four ships helped them skirt the worst terrain, but they drove through Australia, India, the Middle East and across the rugged Alps of southern Europe. It was a massive effort.

To end their journey, Riley entered them in the second Monte Carlo Rally— a reliability time and distance event starting from a choice of nineteen locations converging on Monaco, with points awarded on degree of difficulty. Richmond drove from Palermo in Sicily, covered 1788 kilometres in 51 hours and finished seventeenth in the small-car class.

At a gala welcome dinner in London, Richmond sat next to Arthur Waite. Waite strongly urged Victor Riley, one of the brothers who ran the Riley Motor Company, to find a car for Joan to race in Britain and on the continent.

The Brooklands 1000—held over two days because drivers did not race at night—was like two grands prix strung together. Richmond survived a lurid spin when a tie rod broke. '[World land speed record holder] John Cobb in the Talbot was close behind and a terrible crash seemed imminent but Cobb, thankfully, missed me,' she recalled. Richmond and Wisdom averaged 141.59 km/h on the combined banked and road circuit, and Joan was at the wheel at the finish. 'I didn't know if we were still leading until I saw Arthur Waite with the chequered flag and then I knew we'd won,' she later recalled. 'I drove, terribly excited, back to the pits where Elsie climbed in. At the official enclosure, we were surrounded by people who garlanded us with flowers and pulled us out of the car and hugged us. In those days, the cars leaked oil and combined with the dirt and dust from the tyres and the track, one really looked a sight.'

Richmond—tall, slim, elegant—was at home with the British aristocracy. Her new fame brought her driving offers and suitors. She drove for Riley, Singer, Triumph, MG, Aston Martin, HRG, and she raced a three-litre open-wheel Ballot previously campaigned by the great Sir Malcolm Campbell.

In 1937, aged 32, Joan met London stockbroker Bill Bilney and took him racing. She'd already been to the Le Mans 24 Hour race with the works MG team and finished 24th. Now she came back with Bilney in a self-prepared special-bodied Ford 10. It was a step down from her works drives, but the couple brought it home fourteenth.

Joan invited Bill to join her as co-driver in a works AC sports car at the Donington Park 12 Hour race for sports cars. The track had recently been built in rural Leicestershire, squeezing through thick old stone arches and around solid stone walls. It would soon be the scene of British motor racing's greatest pre–World War II humiliation, when Germany's Auto Union Silver Arrows would clean up in the British Grand Prix. On the eve of the 12 Hour race, Bill asked Joan to marry him and she agreed.

'Our idea for the race was that I, being the more experienced, would take the first part, Bill would relieve me for the middle and then I would take over again,' Joan recalled. 'It was still wet when I handed over to Bill. He tried to overtake a Riley Nine, the two cars locked wheels together and crashed at full speed into

Bill Bilney, who had become Joan Richmond's fiancé the night before, died when the AC they were sharing was crushed by another car against the unforgiving brick wall of the Donington circuit in 1937, on the infamous Holly Wood section of the track. The other driver involved, S.H. Robinson, escaped with a broken leg.

a stone wall. The impact was terrific, the AC was crushed between the wall and Bill was killed. The ambulance took him to hospital in Derby, but we knew he was dead. I was completely shattered. To this day, I blame myself for asking Bill to drive with me.'

Joan lived through the Blitz in London in World War II, and sailed for Melbourne on 27 March 1946. The war had taken its toll. Joan took up residence for a while at Melbourne's Windsor Hotel, and entered the post-war revival meeting at Mount Panorama in October 1946, but did not race. She died, aged 94, in 1999. Many of her trophies and memorabilia are in the National Museum of Australia collection in Canberra.

Joan Richmond: surely a motorsport hero deserving greater recognition. In 2021 there were strong suggestions she should be inducted into the Australian Motorsport Hall of Fame.

3

OUR FIRST FORMULA ONE 'ACE'
Tony Gaze

TONY GAZE WAS THE REAL DEAL—AUSTRALIA'S FIRST Formula One driver in its professional era and its very last amateur hero. He bridged the gap between the old world and the new—not only for Australia but for the emboldened and ambitious world of Formula One.

Who could be better? Here was a genuine World War II fighter ace—decorated not once but three times for bravery in battle; a skilled warrior, whose actions defined coolness and calm under pressure; and a man who conducted his life with exemplary dignity.

Gaze and his good friend, 1938 Australian Grand Prix winner Peter Whitehead, were never destined to become Formula One professionals. The discipline imposed by the works teams, meant for younger and hungrier men, was not necessarily to their liking.

The factories knew that. They needed privateers like Gaze and Whitehead as customers, not as employees. Customers enriched the cash flow of the works teams, as well as filling out the grids. Occasionally, they might even add to a team's winning tally. They were, in the 1950s, an essential act in the circus of Formula One.

Tony Gaze, in his HWM-Alta F2 car with its green-and-gold stripes, was the first Australian to race in a world championship grand prix. HW Motors entered four works F2 cars in the 1952 Belgian Grand Prix. Tony's year-older version was the fifth HWM F2 in the field. Gaze outqualified one of the works cars and, as the last car classified as a finisher, was the fourth of the HWMs home.

Tony Gaze OAM DFC** was an Australian Spitfire ace in World War II and our first Formula One driver in the FIA world championship era. He referred to himself as 'almost unknown'. The cars he raced and the planes he flew have become incredibly valuable: in 2015 a Supermarine Spitfire fetched £3.1 million [A$5.7 million] at auction; Tony's own HWM Alta racing car secured £169,500 [A$311,694] a year later.

Tony Gaze contested four world championship grands prix. It was a limited campaign, but he was racing against the best in the world.

It helps to have money. Frederick Anthony Owen Gaze, born in Melbourne in 1920, was okay in that department. His Scottish grandfather had property and retail investments and 'interests in gold'. His father, Irvine, joined Ernest Shackleton's third (unsuccessful) Antarctic expedition, and fought in the Great War, flying Bristol fighters for the Royal Flying Corps. He married Freda Sadler, whose parents owned tracts of land and the Westhampnett Mill adjacent to the Duke of Richmond's Goodwood estate in Sussex.

Young Tony went to school at exclusive Geelong Grammar (Prince Charles was later sent there) and went up to Cambridge, from where, at eighteen, he raced his uncle's Hudson at the Brooklands speed bowl, just for fun, and enrolled in the RAF as soon as World War II hostilities began.

In the next four years, Tony Gaze was attributed with 12.5 enemy kills—the tenth-highest of all Australians in the conflict—all of them in Spitfires. His last kill was on 30 April 1945, the day Adolf Hitler suicided in his Berlin bunker. Tony had been shot at several times (bullet holes in the wings were a regular feature of his flights back from battle) and he was shot down once in France. With the help of the French Resistance he returned to Britain, hiking over the Pyrenees into Spain.

He won the Distinguished Flying Cross three times—once for taking out two German planes on the tail of his flight leader, and once for becoming the first Allied pilot to shoot down a German jet, the Me 262. He was one of the first to fly the Allies' jet-powered Gloster Meteor.

He'd flown with the greats—Wing Commander Douglas 'Tin Legs' Bader, Allied ace Johnnie Johnson (38 kills), even Colonel Paul Tibbets, the American who piloted the *Enola Gay* when it dropped the atomic bomb on Hiroshima.

At the beginning, Tony's younger brother Scott had joined him in pilot training, and they'd arranged to join 610 Squadron flying out of the Goodwood estate, quite close to their grandfather's ancestral home. They drove down in their sports cars: Tony in a smart little MG J2 with aero screens, cycle guards and leather bonnet strap (later to be replaced by a drophead Aston Martin); Scott in his somewhat more staid Alvis. But on 23 March 1941, their flights went in search of Junkers Ju 88 bombers over the English Channel and, of the two brothers, only Tony returned. Scott, just turned nineteen, was never found.

The Gaze family, particularly Tony, made a big impression on the Dukes of Richmond. Later when their WWII airstrip became the Goodwood motor race

track, they honoured Tony's young brother. In the study of Lord March—the current Duke of Richmond—is a small trophy topped with a model of a Spitfire, its propeller still able to be turned. It is the Scott Gaze Memorial Challenge Trophy and for many years it was given to the first British driver to complete the British Grand Prix.

Tony was 25 when the war ended, and the question was: 'What next?'

Motor racing—speed and danger—provided the obvious substitute.

'Tony was always just my grandpa,' said Will Davison, twice winner of the Bathurst 1000 and a third-generation member of the motor-racing dynasty started by four-times Australian Grand Prix champion Lex Davison. 'Lex had died in 1965 in his Brabham Climax at Melbourne's Sandown race track and by the time I was born [in 1982], my grandmother Diana, Lex's widow, had already been married to Tony for five years. Tony and Di were always my grandparents. Lex was the legend.'

Tony had become the step-patriarch of the Davison family, an inspiration to a trio of young tearaways—Will, Alex and their cousin James, who went on to success in Australia, Europe and America.

He taught the boys so much—lessons from his wartime experiences that applied also to motor racing: 'At dinner, he'd shuffle off to bring back this big, brown box full of photographs and his memories and then he'd just talk,' Will said. '"Always polish your aeroplane; it's good for an extra ten knots."' Throughout the war, while his fellow pilots were playing cards, waiting for the call to scramble, Tony would be at his Spitfire, polishing and repolishing it. It became an obsession. After a while he started to fill in the panel gaps, smoothing the surface. When he shot down the Me 262 it was because his was the only Spitfire that could keep pace with the jet—and it surprised the Germans as much as it did his own squadron.

He taught the Davison boys about early aerodynamics. When the Germans invaded Britain with their V-1 buzz bombs—pilotless missiles that came in low and fast at 550 km/h—one strategy was to get up really close, placing your wingtips just a few centimetres beneath the missile, then flick your wing upward

Aerodynamics of the most precise and precarious form. During World War II, Tony Gaze would manoeuvre his Spitfire's wing under the winglets of the German V-1 buzzbombs—'doodlebugs'—to throw the bombs off their trajectories. On 8 August 1944, flying his Spitfire XIV for the RAF's 610 Squadron, Tony destroyed a doodlebug en route to London off Beachy Head, East Sussex.

to upset the bomb's gyroscope, sending it spiralling off course. It took precision and more than a modicum of bravery to accomplish that manoeuvre. Tony had been credited with V-1 kills.

Tony Gaze married well, post-war. In 1944 he had met Kay Wakefield, widow of British motor-racing champion Johnny Wakefield, who'd died flying a Supermarine Spitfire, the Navy version. Kay's family was big in printing, publishing and engineering. Johnny had also left a considerable fortune. The family estate,

Caradoc Court in Herefordshire, provided ample opportunity for developing a motor-racing stable.

Gaze is credited with turning Westhampnett airfield into the renowned Goodwood Motor Circuit. He'd known the Duke of Richmond, Lord Freddie March—a racing enthusiast and president of the Junior Car Club—throughout the war. When the Duke was looking for a racetrack for his club, Tony pointed out that many of the RAF chaps had been using his own perimeter taxiways for exactly that purpose. The Goodwood press room is named the Tony Gaze Building, in recognition of his suggestion. The first Goodwood race meeting was held in 1948, and the first 500cc race was won by debutant Stirling Moss.

Gaze was back in Australia by then, racing his British-built Formula Two 2-litre Alta in his one and only Australian Grand Prix appearance. The wide-open airfield of Point Cook outside Melbourne was the venue, but Gaze's car had been handicapped out of contention and he retired after five laps with electrical problems. For fun, he had become the Australian importer of HRG, another race car built by the British garagistes, and he sold them to people like Stan Jones, winner of the 1959 Australian Grand Prix and father of 1980 world champion Alan Jones; and Bib Stillwell, who became four-time Australian champion. You could buy an HRG as a sports car or stripped down to become a monoposto racer.

Lex and Diana Davison became close friends of Tony and Kay Gaze. Lex bought several of Tony's race cars and used one, an HWM Jaguar, to win the 1954 Australian Grand Prix. It was a grand life, full of laughter, high jinks and good racing. But it wasn't Europe. Tony and Kay returned in style to the UK by ship and bought a new Formula Two Alta. Tony used it to settle into the Continental rhythm of racing, claiming a few non-championship victories. He travelled with his own mechanic. He'd given the chap a choice: be paid a mechanic's wages, or work for no money and live with Tony and Kay at Caradoc Court, travelling all-expenses-paid on the Continent. He made the lifestyle decision.

Their campaign was so successful that in 1952 it seemed logical to step up to the world championship. Grands prix lived up to their name—massive events of up to 500 kilometres and time-certain at three hours. On 22 June 1952, Tony Gaze became the first Australian to enter a world championship grand prix.

The car was an HWM Formula Two, the ex-Stirling Moss 1951 works machine, in national colours—British racing green. Gaze felt it necessary to represent Australia, so he painted a gold stripe across the cowl in front of the windscreen. Strictly speaking it was against the rules. He told scrutineers he'd had a methanol spill and, without having the matching green paint to repair the damage, he'd applied the gold band.

In its formative years, the FIA championship allowed lesser-powered Formula Two cars to compete in their Formula One races. It helped fill out the field and there were circuits on which the F2 cars were highly competitive. The daunting high-speed Spa-Francorchamps track in the Ardennes forest of Belgium was not one of them. In his debut world championship grand prix there, Gaze qualified sixteenth from twenty-two starters and finished fifteenth.

From the start, a fuel leak sprayed methanol in his face, with no closed-face helmet to guard him. Methanol is highly toxic. Ingested, it can kill you. In your eyes, it can blind you. Wisely, he pulled into the pits but only to repair the pump.

When he rejoined, it was raining and the wet weather was his friend. He skidded and slipped his way up through the field, but with a lap to go, a bird flew into his face. (Eight years later, British driver Alan Stacey would die at the same circuit from bird strike.) 'I got double vision,' Gaze told his biographer Stewart Wilson. 'I put my hand up and saw flesh and blood and thought, "My God, that's my eye!", but it was only the guts of the bird.'

Tony crawled to the finish, passed by several of the cars he'd overtaken, to finish six laps behind the winning works Ferrari 500 of Alberto Ascari, who would be crowned world champion that year.

A month later, at the British Grand Prix at Silverstone, Gaze qualified 26th of 32 on the fast, flat track. An oil pipe burst, but when he pulled to the pits for repairs, officials would not let him rejoin without re-scrutineering the car for safety. He'd lost too much time and retired.

The never-ending sweeping curves of Germany's Nürburgring (more than 170 of them on the long Nordschleife circuit) suited him better. He qualified fourteenth of 30 starters, an excellent result. And he was passing cars, too, when he speared off the road on the exit to the left-hand concrete-banked Karussell. He recovered then went off on the next corner too. The rear axle had broken, making the car undriveable.

Monza in September that year was heartbreaking. The HWMs were not fast enough to qualify in their own right but Gaze hatched a plan: 'I saw Alberto Ascari in the Ferrari coming up behind me at the Curva Grande and I thought if I could stay in front of him through the Lesmo curves until the start of the back straight I could get a tow and I'd certainly qualify.'

But he lost control in the second Lesmo, almost taking out the world champion elect. Afterwards: 'I went over to him and apologised. I don't think anyone had done that before because he slapped me on the back and said: "Okay now we go and have a cup of tea."'

Officials stand over Gaze's car in the 1952 British Grand Prix, refusing to let it go back out on track, and classifying Gaze as a non-finisher on lap 19 of 82. Gaze had again outqualified one of the HWM works team, this time Lance Macklin.

Ferrari excited and disappointed Gaze. In 1954, Enzo Ferrari offered him an ex-works Formula One car for the world championship season. The first person to whom he had sold a race car was Tony's wealthy friend, Peter Whitehead. Whitehead had rewarded Ferrari with a win in the 1949 Czech Grand Prix, and he'd found favour with Maranello, the manufacturing base of Ferrari and the spiritual home of the brand.

It was natural that Gaze and Whitehead—two kindred privateer spirits—would form an unofficial team.

Ferrari said he was prepared to sell them two 3-litre Ferrari 500s for non-championship races in Australia, New Zealand and South Africa, then convert them to the specification of the new 2.5-litre world title regulations so

Tony Gaze and Peter Whitehead campaigned their identical works Ferraris in Queenshaven, South Africa, in 1955 and in New Zealand in 1956. Whitehead won the Lady Wigram Trophy on the airfield outside Christchurch, with Gaze 18 seconds behind in second position.

they could contest the 1955 F1 championship. It was a sensational opportunity. Gaze's car was the Ferrari 500 in which Ascari had won back-to-back titles in 1952 and 1953.

The Down Under summer season was as happy as could be. Whitehead was second in New Zealand with Gaze third. Whitehead won Australia's South Pacific Championship, with Gaze third again. Then Gaze won in South Africa and they sent the Ferraris back to Maranello for conversion as agreed.

But Enzo Ferrari refused. Ferrari had come under immense world championship pressure from the works Mercedes team, and perhaps he wanted to devote all his attention to his works effort. He offered no explanation—just refused to do the work. Gaze would not contest another world championship race. Most likely he and Whitehead were bruised and annoyed, but you wouldn't know it. They were too busy having fun.

They'd turned their attention to sports cars and rallying. Gaze joined Lex Davison and Stan Jones to drive an FJ Holden in the Monte Carlo Rally. They came home 64th and Holden was so pleased it gave each of them a new car. Gaze became a member of the Kangaroo Stable—a group of Australians that campaigned three Aston Martin DB3 sports across Europe in 1955.

At year's end, Gaze and Whitehead returned to Australasia with their Ferraris. They followed Stirling Moss home in the 1956 New Zealand Grand Prix and then, after Moss left for the UK, took turns to share victories in another three New Zealand races. Back in Australia, Tony sold his Ferrari to Lex Davison, who used it to win the Australian Grand Prix in 1957 and 1958.

In 1958, Peter Whitehead and his brother plunged their 3.4-litre Jaguar sedan off a bridge in Lasalle, while contesting the Tour de France Automobile, and Peter was killed. Gaze kept a promise he'd made to Kay to finally retire from a sport in which, suddenly, too many people were dying. He tried salmon fishing on their estate, then world championship sailplaning. He represented Australia in the 1960 world gliding titles.

In 1976, Kay Gaze died after complications from hip replacement surgery. They'd not had children and Tony returned to Australia. On 14 July 1977 he married Diana Davison, matriarch of the Davison dynasty.

It was 2008 at the annual—and, as it turned out near-final—Speed on Tweed, an ambitious gathering of the very best historic racing cars of Australia's past, held at Murwillumbah on the north coast of New South Wales. An old man, grey-haired, was stooped over a front-engine HWM Alta. 'Moss reckoned I got it wrong,' Tony Gaze was saying to his grandson Will Davison. He was lost in the moment: back at Goodwood, 1954, at the bottom of Lavant Straight heading into Woodcote. 'It was the pedals, you see. The accelerator was in the middle with the clutch on the left and the brake on the far right. Moss reckoned I trod on the middle one, thinking it was the brake. Anyway, it wasn't going to stop so I spun it, hit a bank, flew in the air and wrote it off.' His recounting was full of the privateer's derring-do.

At his grandfather's instructions, young Will, once a Formula One aspirant himself, climbed on board to confirm the pedal box layout. He nodded in the affirmative and they both burst out laughing.

Diana died on 6 August 2012. Tony Gaze, awarded a Medal of the Order of Australia (OAM) for his contribution to motorsport, followed on 29 July 2013.

4

THE BENCHMARK
Jack Brabham

JACK BRABHAM—AUSTRALIA'S MOST SUCCESSFUL
Formula One driver ever—created a massive rod for his own back: 'I try to win at the slowest possible speed,' he said. It was an engineer's statement, an indication of mechanical sympathy by placing the least amount of necessary stress on the car. And yet with that simple philosophy—which he espoused but did not always practise—he branded his legacy as a driver in Formula One at a level beneath the all-time gods of speed.

One unguarded comment can define your place in history, even if it's not true. Jack did that to himself as a driver, but not as an engineer. His unique place in Formula One has been cemented because Jack is the only driver ever to win a Formula One World Drivers' Championship in a car of his own making. It's an accomplishment that will never be repeated.

Grand prix history reveres the bold and the swift. Brabham's name seldom appears on lists of the most poles or fastest laps, or even lists of the most notable drivers. The record books present him as nothing more than relentless: just 261 championship points collected over sixteen seasons; ten fastest laps and thirteen pole positions in his entire career; 32 visits to the podium and fourteen wins.

When champagne was for more than simply spraying: Jack Brabham after his win at the 1966 French Grand Prix. It was his first grand prix victory in his own Repco Brabham, the first time any driver had won in a car of his own manufacture, and his first win in six years, since Portugal in 1960.

But these results netted him three World Drivers' Championships and two World Constructors' Championship titles. And that's the point—the bland record totally misrepresents the man. 'Black Jack was a fierce competitor, an outstanding engineer, a tiger of a driver, an excellent politician and a hands-on creator and visionary,' US legend Dan Gurney said when Brabham passed away on Australia's Gold Coast in 2014, aged 88.

Gurney had won the Brabham Formula One team's first championship grand prix, at Rouen in 1964. Two years later he'd gone his own way to try to emulate the boss: 'I followed the trail Jack had blazed by trying to build, race and win with my own F1 cars,' Gurney said. 'Only three men in the history of auto racing have managed to do that. Bruce McLaren and I won races'—one grand prix win each, both in the Belgian GP a year apart—'but Jack won world championships. He will be forever in a class all by himself.'

It's time to set the record straight on Brabham's speed, too. 'He was deceptively fast,' three-time world champion Sir Jackie Stewart wrote. 'He was one of the most difficult men to overtake—never seemingly blocking intentionally but somehow he was incredibly difficult to overtake.'

Jack's speedway background created habits he was loath to break: 'Jack was famous for putting a wheel off the circuit on the exit of a corner to spray dirt and stones at any following driver, especially if they happened to be getting close,' twice Australian Gold Star champion Spencer Martin, a driver who stayed home while others trod the European path, said. 'Knowing a stone could break your goggles and cause serious eye injury, I wasn't happy.'

Martin's mentor, David McKay, was not happy with Jack either. In 2004, the first Australian Touring Car champion, Australian Sports Car champion and nearly the 1961 Australian Grand Prix champion was dying of melanoma-induced cancer. Typically, he'd taken charge of his own funeral arrangements and had limited mourners to 100. Brabham was not among them; in fact, he was deliberately excluded. 'He's taken enough from me,' was McKay's response to his funeral organisers. Brabham was as tough a negotiator off track as he was a competitor, and McKay, a Brabham customer and no shrinking violet himself in a financial tussle, had a long memory. It's doubtful Brabham would have been too perturbed. 'I'm going to die without an enemy in the world,' he joked a decade later, just before his own death. 'I'm going to outlive the bastards.'

In 1978 Jack Brabham, unhappily retired, received a brown envelope in the mail: 'It was from the Australian government inviting me to accept a knighthood.' (Although the Australian honours system was inaugurated in 1976, it overlapped

Typical Jack Brabham body language—hunched over the wheel, so different to the laidback style of his competitors, a legacy of his speedway background. By 1967, Jack was a three-time world champion. He'd claimed pole position for that year's Monaco Grand Prix, but his Repco engine blew on the first lap. Two engine failures that season arguably cost him his fourth world title.

with British imperial recognition for some time.) He would be the first of six world Formula One luminaries to be knighted over the next 43 years, a pathfinder again, ahead of drivers Jackie Stewart, Stirling Moss and Lewis Hamilton, and team owners Frank Williams and Patrick Head.

'For me it was recognition of what Australians can achieve for their national pride through motorsport,' Jack said. He was being a bit disingenuous. The gong took the edge off the pain he was suffering from having retired 'way too early', but no way could you get away with calling him Sir Jack—that was a bit too obvious.

'My father was not likely to go out and celebrate. The best you'd get out of him when he got home would be "job well done",' said Geoffrey Brabham, Le

Mans 24 Hour winner, multiple US Sports Car (IMSA) champion, and the eldest of Jack and Betty's three sons. He enjoyed the most unusual of childhoods. Jack left Betty and Geoff in Australia in 1955 when he went to see what the UK had to offer. He came back to collect them in 1956.

For the next fifteen years, Geoff became his father's sidekick at the motor races. Betty tended to stay home, especially after sons Gary and David were born. 'It just seemed normal to me, but when I started going to a small boarding school, Northease Manor in Sussex, and the boys were talking about what they'd done on the weekend and I'd say I was at the German or Italian grands prix, the penny dropped,' Geoff smiled down the phone from his COVID-19 isolation in Indianapolis, a long way from the Brabham home on the Gold Coast.

'We'd go to those fly-away races in his own aircraft and sometimes it would just be Dad and me. Other times he'd offer people lifts. We'd land in paddocks beside the racetrack—everyone did it. I recall when [Lotus boss] Colin Chapman ground-looped his plane and collapsed the undercarriage. Everyone cheered.'

Flying influenced Geoff's young mind, even more than Formula One. 'One of the reasons [Jack] was so good was because he had an intuitive feel for everything mechanical. We were flying into Luton airfield, just him and me, and there was a pea-soup fog. They redirected us to two other airfields, but they were closed too and then they said, "Head for Europe." But Dad told them we didn't have enough fuel and they'd have to talk us down. There was no panic, he was under control, and then they said, "You *could* be over the runway now"—and he just pulled back the throttles and we touched the ground. There's not a person in the world I would rather have been sitting next to than him.'

In October 1970, Geoff travelled with Jack to his father's last ever grand prix. It was Mexico, the crowd was manic, and Jack's last race ended in a DNF (did not finish). Geoff had the presence of mind to take the steering wheel from the car before it was souvenired by a spectator. It's in his home study today.

'Well, what do we do now?' father said to son. It was an incredibly serious question, especially from a bloke who seldom asked for personal advice.

Jack Brabham had a career in two parts. He won two consecutive world championships with the Cooper Car Company—the first team and the first driver to win a world title with a rear-engine F1 car. Then his own Brabham cars won two successive world championships, the first with Jack at the wheel, the second with New Zealand's Denny Hulme.

His early influence was Don Bain, winner of the Junior and Senior Tourist Trophies in 1931 and 1937 on the old Vale circuit at Bathurst. Bain was his boss

Mexico, 1970: Jack Brabham's last Formula One world championship race. His Brabham BT33 led Denny Hulme's McLaren M14A, but then suffered engine failure. Hulme finished third and claimed fourth in the world title. Brabham was classified fifth in his last world championship, equal with Jackie Stewart.

in RAAF flight maintenance towards the end of World War II. Brabham built and raced his own midget speedcar, won the Australian Speedcar title at Sydney Royale in 1948 and moved on to tar-track racing. He made the transition in the 1951 Australian Hill Climb Championship at Rob Roy in Victoria, which he won using his speedway midget fitted with four-wheel brakes to comply with regulations. Brabham's exceptional talent made him a drawcard and promoters paid him an appearance fee—they called it 'travel money'. Jack and his father Tom, a well-to-do Sydney wholesale greengrocer, bought a Cooper Bristol race car, the first to be brought to Australia. The Brabhams had money for just half and they persuaded oil additive company REDeX to fund the rest in return for naming rights.

Almost where it all started. Brabham, a speedway champion, upgraded to a Cooper Bristol, bought in 1953 from a deceased estate. The car—known as the REDeX Special—was the springboard for the country's most successful world champion.

The REDeX Special is part of Australian motor-racing folklore. Advertising on cars was banned and the governing body—the Confederation of Australian Motor Sport (CAMS)—cautioned them for breaking the rules. To appease them, Brabham taped brown paper over the REDeX sign, which blew off with the first assault of speed, creating controversy. 'Legend has it that CAMS' attitude to sponsorship was the trigger that caused me to head for Europe,' Jack said. 'More likely if REDeX had withdrawn its sponsorship it would have been the trigger that stopped me motor racing.' At the New Zealand Grand Prix in late 1954, the secretary of Britain's Royal Automobile Club, Dean Delamont, told Brabham a better future awaited him in the UK.

Jack hopped on a Qantas Super Constellation—a big deal in those days—and gave himself a few scant months to suss out the UK scene.

The Cooper Car Company in Surbiton had led the post-war rear-engine revolution with its sensational 500cc Formula Three cars, which provided a launching point for the careers of drivers like Stirling Moss, Mike Hawthorn and Peter Collins. Brabham was aware of the benefits of rear-engine cars. Back in Australia, his friend Ron Tauranac had been building and racing a very effective rear-engine special. He called it the RALT—from the initials of Ron and his brother, Austin Lewis Tauranac. (They'd added Austin's middle name so the car wouldn't be called the RAT.)

In the UK, Jack became a serial pest at Coopers. He persuaded John Cooper and his father Charlie to let him build a car larger than the F3, based on Cooper's sports car, with an enveloping body and a 2-litre six-cylinder Bristol engine behind

Jack Brabham in his first Formula One world championship race, the 1955 British Grand Prix, driving his self-built T39 'Bobtail' Cooper Bristol. He brought two T39s back to Australia—one for himself, with which he won the Australian Grand Prix, and the other for Bill Patterson, who became the 1961 Australian Gold Star champion.

the driver. He finished it the night before the 1955 British Grand Prix at Aintree. It was his first entry in a world championship race, and he qualified last. The hurriedly prepared car failed him on lap 30 of 90, while Moss won on Mercedes. Jack raced on, though, in non-championship events, keeping close company with Moss. Their duels were acclaimed by enthusiastic media.

At season's end he brought the 'bobtail' Cooper back to Australia and won the Australian Grand Prix at Adelaide's Port Wakefield street circuit, the first win for a rear-engine car in the title race. Local media said the 'bobtail' resembled not so much a works car as an Australian special—built in England. Brabham began a tradition of disposing of his cars in Australia—he sold the Cooper to Victorian car dealer and sometime racer Reg Smith (who was killed in 1960, in a fiery crash at Mount Panorama in a GT championship race) and returned to the UK with a 'brown paper bag full of cash'.

Brabham was a late starter. He was twenty before he raced a car, 30 in his first world championship season, and 33 when he won his first of two world championships for Cooper. 'You're going to be a works driver,' Charlie Cooper told him. 'You get to drive the truck. If you get to the track in time you can drive the spare car, too.'

It was John Cooper who gave Brabham his sobriquet 'Black Jack'. Brabham went on record in CAMS' 60th anniversary book: 'It wasn't because of my dark hair, my five o'clock shadow or my attitude. It was because John reckoned I came from Black Fella country. You can't say that these days, but that's how it happened.'

Brabham contributed as much to Cooper's world championship success as a constructor as he did as a driver. His machining skills complemented those of Owen 'The Beard' Maddock, Cooper's designer since 1950. Brabham enhanced Maddock's design, and he called on Ron Tauranac in Australia to draw and manufacture components.

The Coventry Climax engine, which had been designed as a stationary power unit for firefighting equipment, was Cooper's ace. It was lightweight, providing the Cooper with an extremely advantageous power-to-weight ratio. On tight circuits it was a rocket ship.

In May 1957, at the Monaco Grand Prix, in only his second world championship grand prix start, Brabham worked his way up to third from fifteenth, slipping and sliding the tiny Cooper through spaces that drivers of larger cars couldn't access. His aggressive drive was the race highlight. Five laps from home, the Cooper stopped; a high-pressure aeronautical fuel pump had vibrated loose. Brabham pulled off his crash hat and goggles and pushed the car 800 metres to the finish,

Original Aussie grit: Jack Brabham would never give up. He pushed his fuel-starved T43 Cooper Climax to sixth in the 1957 Monaco Grand Prix, then pushed again in the 1959 US Grand Prix at Sebring, this time to confirm his first world championship title.

even through the tunnel with winner Juan Fangio's Maserati flashing perilously by in the half-light. He was sixth—last, as it turned out. But two years later he'd push again, on the day he won the world championship.

It was the 1959 US Grand Prix on the Sebring airstrip circuit in Florida—hot, flat and flat-out. Brabham had won the world F2 championship for Cooper the year before with young Bruce McLaren, his New Zealand protégé, second. Now, with wins at Monaco and the British Grand Prix, plus three other podiums, he was leading the nine-round F1 title. Tony Brooks on Ferrari and Stirling

Right number—different car. Jack Brabham on three wheels under Sebring's MG bridge, pursued by Bruce McLaren. The night before the 1959 world championship-deciding US Grand Prix, Brabham swapped Cooper Climaxes with McLaren. Jack's Cooper had been overheating and he didn't trust it to run race distance. As it turned out, his replacement car ran out of fuel and Bruce won the race, but the championship went to Jack.

Moss on Cooper were both in contention. Never in the ten-year history of the championship had it been so close.

Moss broke down; but Brooks was closing. Teammate McLaren shepherded Brabham in the lead. Then, with half a lap to go the Cooper ran out of fuel, clumsily—though accidentally—under-fuelled by John Cooper. McLaren almost stopped to help. That would have been a huge error. Brabham needed to keep the fast-closing Brooks down the finishing order. He urgently waved Bruce on and he became the youngest ever winner of a world championship grand prix at the time.

'I thought of Monaco '57,' Brabham said. 'I scrambled out, wrenched off my helmet and goggles and began to push. Tony [Brooks] slammed past, then I just got my head down, put my back into the job, and kept on pushing.' Motorcycle police came from the pits to give him an escort. Dean Delamont desperately held them and others back; outside assistance would have disqualified him.

Brooks passed Brabham to come third, but it was not enough. He needed a win to claim the title. Jack Brabham had become Australia's first Formula One world champion.

In April 1960, Ron Tauranac arrived at Heathrow Airport. Jack Brabham had sent him a return air ticket, which he'd converted into one-way fare so he could afford to bring his wife Norma and daughter Jann too. Brabham was at odds with Charlie Cooper, and he'd imported Tauranac right under Cooper's nose.

Charlie had been well satisfied with the 1959 world title and wanted to change nothing on the car for 1960. John Cooper and Brabham knew that was madness. Lotus would launch its first rear-engine car that year and a major rule change in 1961 meant others, including Ferrari, would follow. Brabham put up a major smokescreen. Ostensibly Tauranac would work for Brabham's new retail car business, modifying limited-edition road cars for the Rootes Group. Beneath a cloak of secrecy, though, he was available to help with work on the 1960 entrant.

Brabham and John Cooper set up a virtual skunkworks to build the 1960 'Lowline' Cooper T53. It was only when it was rolled out as a fait accompli that it received Charlie's grudging consent. His praise was more glowing when Brabham again won the Drivers' and Constructors' World Championships for Cooper in 1960. Ron Tauranac, Brabham said, 'had design input into the car's new coil spring rear end'. It was, according to Brabham, 'the first really good race car Cooper had produced'. Brabham won five grands prix in succession and sealed the title long before the circus arrived in the United States for the final round. This time, John Cooper overfuelled the car and it caught fire.

'We would always try to sell our cars in Australia,' Brabham told me much later. 'We would come out for the Tasman Series'—a counter-seasonal summer series that gave the Europeans a place to race in the Northern Hemisphere winter—'and we'd leave our cars behind with the locals and go home with a big

Jack Brabham (Lowline T53 Cooper Climax) leads Stirling Moss (Lotus 18 Climax) in the non-championship 1961 Brussels Grand Prix. Brabham and Moss enhanced each other's careers until Moss's near-fatal crash at Goodwood in 1962. In eleven seasons, Moss scored sixteen grand prix wins; in sixteen seasons Brabham claimed two fewer wins, but three championships. 'Jack was the toughest of tough competitors,' Moss said.

bag of cash—and maybe a trophy. But I had to give the money to John Cooper when I got back to the UK. That got me thinking about starting my own team.'

By mid-1961, Motor Racing Developments (MRD), a company owned secretly by Brabham while he was still under contract to Cooper, and Ron Tauranac had built and sold its first open-wheel racing car for the new driver development Formula Junior series. It was bought by Tasmanian Gavin Youl, who brought it home fourth and second in its first two races at Goodwood. That was a good result, especially as Youl was an unknown in Britain.

Brabham's cover had been blown: 'MRD is a little project on which Ron Tauranac, an old friend from Australia, has been working,' he said in a prepared press release. No mention of himself. But later in the release, the 'we' appeared: 'We will be making a few models in kit form for a firm in Australia. The car has had an encouraging start and I must say it's very pleasant to have toys of your own to play with.'

Jack had already told John Cooper that he planned to leave Cooper at the end of the year, but Charlie had been kept in the dark. He was apoplectic. Brabham was accused of industrial espionage: 'He's taken all my good ideas. I've taught him everything he knows.' The 1961 championship season did not go well. New 1.5-litre Formula One rules were in place for the first time and Ferrari had stolen a march with its 190-horsepower (142-kilowatt), 120-degree V6. The British teams, with their four-cylinder and later V8 Climax engines, couldn't match the Italians. Neither Brabham nor Cooper troubled the winner's circle. Jack, the defending world-champion driver, was eleventh; Cooper, the world-champion constructor, was fourth.

'You can't call it MRD,' Swiss journalist Jabby Crombac told Jack and Ron. 'It's pronounced *merde* in French and you'd stand a better chance of picking up French sales if you're not talking that way about your car.' So, they called it Brabham, and B (for Brabham) and T (for Tauranac) would become the prefix on each model's nomenclature. MRD would be the holding company.

In eleven years, MRD constructed 592 race cars, twenty of them Formula One versions. They won two World Drivers' Championships, two World Constructors' Championships and five British F3 championships. Mario Andretti used a Brabham copy, with the partners' permission, to win the 1969 Indianapolis 500.

Brabham's considerable clout as a double world champion had opened the door to Australian engineering company Repco (Replacement Parts Company). He'd been supported by Repco's chairman Sir Charles 'Dave' McGrath since the 1950s and, as Repco expanded internationally, the association was good for them both. Brabham's early cars were prepared in a corner of Repco's British outpost. Repco was super-tuning the Coventry Climaxes for Brabham's cars.

In 1966, Brabham and Repco made history. Formula One rules had changed yet again, doubling the allowable cubic capacity to 3 litres. Coventry Climax had pulled out. Jack proposed that Repco build a whole new engine.

McGrath took the pitch forcefully to his board. The window would be open for only a short time, he said, and he was right. By mid-1967, Ford would have empowered English designers Mike Costin and Keith Duckworth, co-founders of Cosworth, to build their response: the Ford DFV (double four valve). It would become the most successful Formula One engine of all time, with 155 wins. But for 1966, there was the potential for a relatively small company from Australia to rule the world. In a politically charged atmosphere, genius mechanical engineer Phil Irving was assigned to convert an American stock block V8 into a world championship winner. He built the original engine—lightweight, simple, reliable— then left in a huff. The project continued.

Brabham and Tauranac were a top team. Brabham had driving skill, mechanical expertise, reputation and, despite his taciturn nature, salesmanship. Tauranac contributed pedantic brilliance as a designer of cars that were well engineered and trustworthy, a rarity in the fragile world of Formula One. It's a pity that for a while the pair didn't really get along.

Ron Tauranac (left) designed cars and built components for Jack Brabham from the beginning of both their careers. Tauranac was made an Officer of the Order of Australia (AO) in recognition of his contribution not only to Brabham but to a succession of motor racers who used his RALTs, designed after Brabham F1 was sold.

In 2021, Ron Tauranac's daughter Jann met with Jack Brabham's grandson Sam at the Historic Sports and Racing Car Association's meeting at Sydney Motorsport Park. Both are seated on Jack and Ron's Brabham BT19—the 1966 world championship-winning car.

Jack Brabham had the mechanical knowledge, and the confidence, to work on his own car—even during a race meeting. Here he adjusts the front suspension of his Brabham BT19 at the 1967 Dutch Grand Prix, in which he came second to Jim Clark, ahead of Denny Hulme.

'Ron was absolutely the only bloke I'd have gone into partnership with,' Brabham said when he sent Tauranac his air ticket. But he treated him mean. MRD wasn't an equal partnership; Brabham held the majority share. And MRD wasn't the race team—it was the car builder. Brabham kept BRO (Brabham Racing Organisation) for himself to run his Formula One program. The accountants advised him to draw only a basic wage from MRD, which meant Ron had to do the same, and he was working for peanuts. At the end of 1965 Ron had had enough, and he told Brabham.

Brabham's response was to look around for an alternative car supplier—BRO wasn't tied to MRD for the supply of its chassis. It could have been a negotiating tactic, it could have been for real, but it was only after Brabham did his due diligence of market opportunity that he and Ron had their face-to-face negotiation. It turned out well. Brabham raised Ron's stake to 50:50 in MRD, and MRD and BRO joined forces on a 50:50 split too. Ron would have a say in the race team as well as the customer car program.

The result was Brabham's third world championship.

But the negotiations had almost fatally delayed car development. Instead of a chassis purpose-built for the Repco engine, Tauranac proposed using the BT19, a small, nimble, lightweight car built to take a 1.5-litre V8 Cosworth engine. Naturally, he strengthened it. Brabham called it the Old Nail.

Brabham came spectacularly good mid-season, just as he had in 1960. The Repco Brabham won four grands prix in succession—in France, Britain, the Netherlands and Germany. The first win in France was historic—the first ever in a grand prix by a driver who was also a constructor. It was also Jack's first F1 victory in six years, since his last with Cooper in 1960.

Jack turned 40 in April 1966. Older men had won world titles but Formula One was increasingly becoming a game for young guns. The media was ribbing him—in truth, it was getting his goat. So, on the grid at Zandvoort for the Dutch Grand Prix, Jack appeared with a long false beard, a walking stick and a stooped back. He climbed with the slow caution of an old man into his car. Then he won the race. He was in the box seat for the world championship title.

It was a busy season.

As well as Repco, Brabham had done a deal with Honda. In 1964, Soichiro Honda hired MRD to help develop its Formula Two program. The Brabham-Hondas, driven by Jack with New Zealand's Denny Hulme riding shotgun in second place (which was written into his contract), swept all before them.

Geoff Brabham flew with Jack to all four winning grands prix. He recalls his father being intent on the Honda association: 'There'd be many Japanese mechanics and engine parts all over the floor of the plane, way above allowable weight.'

Repco, understandably, was able to offer less physical support than the fast-emerging Japanese automotive powerhouse. BRO was recycling and repairing Repco's engines in its own workshop. Tauranac, concerned, was taking their care very seriously. They went to the Italian Grand Prix with a mathematical chance of winning the title, but Brabham retired on lap seven when his engine sprang an oil leak. Ron, obsessed with discovering why, spent the rest of the race with his head in the engine bay. The pair flew home from Monza that night, and there was a media posse waiting at Fairoaks airfield: 'Why are they here?' Tauranac asked. 'Oh, we've won the world championship,' Brabham replied. Tauranac hadn't been watching as John Surtees and Jackie Stewart, the two remaining title contenders, had retired from the race. And they'd not discussed it on the flight back.

With two grands prix still to be run in the season, MRD, BRO and Repco Brabham had made history.

In 1967, Jack Brabham and Denny Hulme each claimed two world Formula One victories. But Hulme visited the podium on eight occasions to Brabham's six. Denny legitimately won his first world championship from his boss. There were just five championship points between them. Repco Brabham won its second World Constructors' Championship.

It was a moment to savour: mid-season, Ford had introduced its Cosworth DFV and Jim Clark had used it in his Lotus 49 to win the last two grands prix of the year, placing third to the Repco Brabham in the championship, a preview of the next season.

The DFV, available to customers at £7000 [A$15,000], would win all but one grand prix in 1968 and it clean swept the field in 1969. Repco tried a comparatively complex four-valve conversion of their engine in 1968 but it was not successful. Repco would not win again, and they withdrew, double world champions, before the 1969 season.

Brabham sold his share of MRD to Ron Tauranac in 1970. He was under increasing family pressure to give away racing altogether. It started with the private testing crash at Silverstone in 1969 when his front left tyre exploded from its rim at 185 km/h and pitched him into a bank. His mechanic, Ron Dennis, had pulled him from that one, when he was trapped by a broken ankle and doused in fuel: 'Ron did a good job to get me out without a spark.' It had been Brabham's only career injury.

So many of his rivals had died. He'd survived a lethal period and for a long time he'd learned how to compartmentalise the consequences.

Opposite: The Repco Brabham engine entered 33 grands prix, won eight of them, and was on the podium 25 times. The small Australian company claimed two World Constructors' Championships and retired from competition at the end of 1968 after just four seasons.

Below: Two world champions in two successive years: Jack Brabham (left) and his employee and teammate Denny Hulme. Hulme's victory was meritorious; he steadfastly supported Brabham throughout his Repco campaign, and claimed his 1967 title while following 'the boss' home.

'He would push the limits, but he always had that feel of where the limit was on any given day. It was the main reason he stayed alive when so many didn't,' Geoff Brabham told me. Way back in 1957, at Reims, he'd tried out a streamlined Cooper F2, wasn't happy with its handling and opted for the normal open-wheeler. Another driver, Bill Whitehouse, begged John Cooper to let him race it.

'I asked Dad, "How did he go?"'

'Well, the car flipped, and he killed himself,' Brabham told his five-year-old son.

Brabham turned 1970 into a valedictory season—driving for Ron Tauranac's team with no pressure as an owner. It started well. He won the South African first round of the title and scored fastest lap. He took fastest lap in four of the first seven grands prix, an indication of his raw speed.

He went to the Indianapolis 500 and was rocketing along, even briefly leading, until his engine broke in two. He was classified thirteenth. Then, at Zandvoort in the Netherlands he was trapped in a crashed car with fuel leaking . . . again. A tyre, once more, had gone down. The family was at the track, including Betty and his father Tom. They intensified their retirement campaign.

The decider came in the British Grand Prix. Jack was still in with a chance of winning his fourth world championship and he was flying, in the lead. But on the last lap—virtually in sight of the chequered flag, he ran out of fuel. Jack hated that human failure so much more than any crash, and it confirmed his decision to quit. For years he blamed Ron Dennis for the fuel. It was three decades before another of the team's mechanics mustered the courage to admit it was his fault. Brabham chuckled about that. He liked the idea of holding Dennis, by then head of McLaren and one of the great success stories of motor racing, accountable.

Jack drove on to the end of the 1970 season. He was lying third in the high-altitude heat of Mexico with the spectators dangerously spilling over onto the track edges when his engine blew just twelve laps from the finish. Geoff, the only family member with him, gathered up his possessions, including his steering wheel, and they headed home, flying commercially.

'I gave up racing far too early,' Brabham told me in our last conversation. 'I got talked into it.' There was nothing pleasant about the way he said it, no casual old-man reminiscences. 'I could have gone on for a few more years.' He pretty much spat the words out.

5

JACK'S THREE SONS
Geoffrey Brabham
Gary Brabham
David Brabham

'I DO NEED TO APOLOGISE THAT THIS SERVICE IS A LITTLE bit late,' Geoffrey Brabham opened his address at his father Jack's funeral in 2014. 'However, [grandsons] Matthew and Sam had racing commitments overseas and I know that Dad would have got out of his coffin and kicked our ass if they missed a couple of races for him. Unfortunately, Matthew lost the Freedom 100 by 5/1000th of a second and Sam managed to roll his car over a couple of times. But Dad would have been proud of them for having a go.' Then he got on with his eulogy.

The Brabhams have always been a racing family. In one year, 1989, Jack's three sons all won major championships: Geoffrey, the IMSA GT sports-car series in the United States; David, the British Formula Three Championship; and Gary, the first British Formula 3000 Championship. They were huge achievements for one family. Jack described himself as a very proud father. 'You're not born a racing driver,' said Geoffrey, adamant. 'It's not genetic—it's a disease. Ability comes from constant exposure.'

Fourteen-year-old Geoffrey Brabham at the 1966 British Grand Prix. Geoff was at his father's side throughout Jack's world championship-winning career. Their bond was absolute.

The family Brabham. Left to right: Betty, youngest son David, Geoffrey, middle son Gary, and Jack. A third generation is now attempting to follow in their tyre tracks.

Betty Brabham had been with Jack from the outset. She'd travelled to early race meetings, riding pillion on his Velocette motorcycle. She'd been with him through his speedway career, worked side by side with him in his engineering shop—not just on racing activities but on customer orders—to help the business succeed. They were a team: 'She used the lathe, making electric motor spindles by the hundred,' Jack said.

But she'd also witnessed death and injury, and it hardened her towards racing. Between 1947 and 1951, Jack's speedway years, eight competitors perished on the Sydney Sports and Showground dirt ovals. In Europe in Formula One, in Jack's active years, there were sixteen race fatalities, and another four drivers died in testing. Betty had seen Jack escape death and she didn't want that for her boys. Betty's dream was that her sons would be brought up in rural Australia, far from motor racing. They bought a 1750-hectare holding outside Wagga Wagga with an 8-kilometre Murrumbidgee River frontage.

Jack tried farming, a car dealership, even an aeronautic business—but he was constantly restless. 'He used aeroplanes like other people use buses,' son Gary said. David, the youngest, was six when they moved back to Australia and onto the farm, the family also maintaining a home in Sydney so Jack could be close to his other interests; Gary was ten. Geoff, nineteen, was of a different generation to his brothers and, like his father, was a seeker of adventure.

GEOFF BRABHAM

Geoffrey, winner of the Le Mans 24 Hour race and multiple US IMSA sports car champion, was the 'practice child'. Just weeks into the family's renewed life in Australia, Geoff discovered a Formula Ford in the workshop of Jack Brabham Ford, the car dealership. It was being driven by local Bob Beasley in the national title.

Jack had reached a very recent covenant with Betty, and with his parents, Tom and May. It didn't include motor racing. Geoff forced his hand. 'It was a struggle,' Geoff said. 'He didn't want me to do it. It took persistence on my part.'

Father and son took the tiny 1600cc racer to nearby Oran Park in 1971 and Geoff steadfastly carved 2 seconds off his lap times to get down to something decent. 'You may as well do a race,' Jack said.

Geoff's first race was at the international circuit at Warwick Farm and Jack went with him. 'The only driving advice my father gave me was, "There's the throttle, brake and steering wheel—if you crash it, don't come back,"' Geoff joked. It was a little more complex than that: 'I think there were times he would have liked to teach me more, but he just didn't know how to put his knowledge into words.'

By 1974, Geoff had won the Australian Formula Two Championship. 'It was my first wings and slicks car,' Geoff said—a car providing track-hugging downforce and mechanical grip. 'Dad tried to overengineer it. It was only when I decided to ignore his advice and simplify things that I started winning races.'

The 1970s were a great time to be young and racing small open-wheelers in Australia. Geoff was racing against drivers who had their eyes on the prize of Formula One, and he was the only one who knew what that meant. But he too was caught up in the buzz and headed for Europe.

Jack gave Geoff workshop space in the car dealership he owned in London, introduced him to fuel supplier ESSO and provided $10,000 seed money. Ron Tauranac was godfather to all three Brabham boys and his RALTs were the chassis of choice for the junior categories. But it all amounted to a bag of beans

Three-year-old Geoffrey Brabham in the pits, in Jack's arms, with Mike Hawthorn, who would go on to win the 1958 world championship—the year before Jack's first win. Geoffrey travelled with his father virtually from the time he was walking. Hawthorn, who famously wore a bow tie while racing, retired at the end of his world championship year and died three months later in a car crash near his home.

alongside the young drivers from Brazil. The money that flowed from them into the UK feeder series was enormous. 'They were testing mid-week, spending what was necessary to be competitive. You had to win seven races in a row just to get recognised,' Geoff said.

Geoff had arrived in the UK with his girlfriend, now wife, Roseina (they'd met at Lakeside Raceway in Queensland in 1974, at a party thrown by racer Bruce Allison—another who'd chance his arm in the UK). They lived in a flat shared by young Aussies in Wimbledon who came and went, all of them equal parts desperately ambitious and poor. It was a Formula One frat house. The place reeked of ambition.

Jack had given him advice: 'There are people who *drive* racing cars, and there are people who *race* racing cars.' In UK F3, they race them. Geoff had not seen anything like it—full grids, separated by milliseconds; cars interlocking wheels; every lap at qualifying speed. The really fast guys were part of works teams with full support systems. Geoff was alone.

He scrambled an eighth in the British Racing Drivers' Club five-round F3 championship and eleventh in the British Automobile Club's twelve-round series. In the circumstances it was an outstanding result.

It took him a year to win a Formula Three round, on the Silverstone Club circuit, and claim a spectacular fourth in the series. 'I felt absolutely alone. One day I was sitting on the grid at a race meeting and the battery lead came off. I had to undo my belt, get out, remove the seat, fix it and repeat the procedure. And it was then I knew I was pissing in the wind.'

Geoff's Formula One dreams were over and he turned to the United States. Jack offered a contact: David Psachie, a fast-talking Learjet salesman from Orange County, California, who 'might' be able to rustle up a deal for Geoffrey to race a Formula Super Vee—effectively a Formula Three car—which was a feeder series to IndyCar.

Next season, 1979, he won the US Super Vee championship, beginning an illustrious career in the United States. He won four IMSA GT sports-car championships for the works Nissan team, was a major contender in the International Race of Champions, and raced in eleven Indianapolis 500s. His best Indy finishes were a fourth and a fifth. In 1993, Peugeot hired him to drive in the Le Mans 24 Hour race, in a French team with two French co-drivers. When it came time to decide which driver would guide the winning car over the finish line, the French team manager Jean Todt, later the president of the FIA, nominated the Australian. It was a mark of respect.

Geoff and Roseina maintain two homes—one on Queensland's Gold Coast, the other at Clearwater Cove, on the lake just north of Indianapolis. The US home is a base for their son Matthew, who is pursuing a motor-racing career. He's won the US F2000 and Pro Mazda championships, and placed 22nd in his only drive in the Indy 500.

In late 2020, father and son went to the Circuit of the Americas, the purpose-built F1 grand prix track in Texas. They drove in the US Vintage National Championship, both in historic Brabham BT35s, and they carved up the field: Matty won; Geoff was second. Jack would have been proud.

In 1958, when Jack Brabham was still a season away from winning his first world championship, six-year-old Geoffrey was already dreaming of his. He got to ride in his dad's Cooper around the pits.

Above: Geoffrey Brabham carved out a strong career in the United States, winning multiple sports car championships and finishing just off the podium in two of his eleven Indianapolis 500s. Here, he drives Danny Sullivan's Team Penske car in practice at the 1989 Indy 500, after Sullivan had broken his wrist.

Right: Geoffrey (centre) was the first of two Brabham brothers to win the Le Mans 24 Hour. He won for Peugeot in 1993, in an otherwise all-French team; David Brabham won for Peugeot in 2009.

GARY BRABHAM

Gary Brabham had a chance to drive for Brabham F1 twice—and both times his father gave the team advice that stopped the deal going ahead. Instead, he 'raced' for one of the most inept teams in Formula One, lasted two events and walked away from Formula One.

Gary raced just two rounds of the 1982 Australian Formula Ford Championship before Jack parachuted him into the 1983 British Formula Ford 2000 Championship. He would drive for Neil Trundle, who'd been a Brabham F1 mechanic alongside Ron Dennis in Jack's day. There couldn't be a better tutor. Gary came eleventh in his first season, sixth in the next.

With his father's backing, he started his own team—Jack Brabham Racing. Life was 'comfortable', compared to the existence Geoff had eked out. There was sponsorship coming in, and he moved up to RALTs in Formula Three: 'I could have come second in the series, but I wrote the car off at Silverstone—head on into the barrier.' Gary went down to his godfather's workshop and built another RALT, then salvaged fifth in the title.

He moved to the just-formed Bowman Automotive team in 1988, came second in the British F3 championship, and at season's end won a F3 Superprix at Brands Hatch that featured 39 of the fastest F3 drivers. The prize was a test in a Benetton Formula One car; instead of merely giving him a test, they turned Gary into a test driver.

'They took me first to Pembrey to work on their rising rate suspension.' Pembrey is a 2.3-kilometre, eight-turn track in Wales renowned as a test and development circuit, and Gary did a good job. His technical feedback impressed the engineers. 'Then we went to Jerez in the south of Spain.' On the wide-open track with huge corners, Gary said his neck 'felt like it was on a bungee cord'. Gary was withstanding 5.5g of force: 'They designed a neck brace, sort of a half-moon behind my head, to keep it upright.'

His hopes of a Formula One race drive were on the rise—perhaps even with Brabham. The team was then owned by Bernie Ecclestone. But Jack let him down. 'I heard third-hand, although Dad never revealed it, that there'd been an opportunity for me to drive the car in the 1989 season,' Gary said. 'But Dad told Bernie I wasn't ready.'

Jack was most likely right. Gary moved to the inaugural British F3000 championships—the new feeder series for Formula One—and won it. His brother, David, who had recently arrived in the UK, took over Gary's Bowman F3 drive and won his championship that year as well.

'That's when I made the stupidest decision of my motor-racing career,' Gary told me. 'I was offered a full works drive by Bridgestone to race F3000 in Japan for a lot of money. But my aim was Formula One. I turned them down. It was an emotional decision, not a business one.'

Japan at the time was a backwater for aspiring racing drivers—but it wouldn't be for long. It soon became a proving ground for drivers with European ambitions. But who was to know?

'I had nothing to drive at all,' Gary said. Then came an approach from Modena-based businessman Ernesto Vita. Vita had secured the rights to a unique W12 'broad arrow' engine designed by Ferrari confidant Franco Rocchi (his engines had won five world championships). It was the most complex engine on the grid, akin to BRM's V16 of 1956, and Gary was part of one of the most disastrous Formula One programs of all time.

Vita called his team 'Life'—the English translation of his surname.

'I didn't have to bring sponsorship—all I had to do was get to the circuits,' Gary said. 'The engine had some potential. It had amazing torque, more than

Opposite: For a while, Gary Brabham had looked like a big chance in Formula One. He'd worked as a test driver for the F1 Benetton team, helping develop the 1989 B189 chassis from the B188—seen here at Jerez in December 1988.

Above: In 1990, Gary Brabham joined the underperforming Life F1 but the car, with its W12 'broad arrow' engine, was a disaster. Brabham struggled through two pre-qualifying sessions before walking away from Formula One.

any other car in the field, but it was totally unreliable.' The car failed to make the grid in any of its fourteen attempts—but Brabham stayed for only two. He managed just four and a half laps in pre-qualifying for the US Grand Prix at Phoenix, the opening race of the season, before the engine blew.

In Brazil, it got worse. The Life did not have a functioning tachometer and the totally disorganised team had turned up without a tyre pressure gauge. Gary borrowed one from the Brabham team, and dropped into Benetton to pick up plates of sandwiches for the Life mechanics because no one had thought to cater for them. The car covered just 400 metres out of the pits before it stopped. 'I flew home the night before the race.'

In mid-1990, Brabham Formula One changed hands again. Its new owner, Japanese billionaire Koji Nakauchi, asked Jack if Gary might be available. 'He told them that to the best of his knowledge I was under contract to Life,' Gary said. Jack was wrong, but Nakauchi's team manager Herbie Blash took him at his word. The team quite liked the idea of a Brabham in a Brabham, so they gave the drive to his younger brother David instead.

Gary's Formula One dreams were over.

The Brabham brothers raced against and with each other in other categories. In the 1990 Macau Grand Prix (the FIA now calls it the F3 World Cup), David won and Gary was sixth. In the Sebring 12 Hour, Gary teamed with Geoff in the works Nissan to win in 1991 and come second in 1992.

But he was losing heart and he withdrew from racing. 'It was too much of a struggle.' He did some high-profile driver training at Brands Hatch, then returned to Australia.

Gary Brabham lives in Brisbane. He has twice been convicted on charges of child sex offences.

His name does not appear on his family's website.

DAVID BRABHAM

On Friday 13 November 1987, on the Adelaide Grand Prix F1 circuit—just two years after the world championship had come to Australia—a remarkable event occurred. David Brabham won the Australian Drivers' Championship.

The Australian Gold Star was the most coveted prize in domestic motorsport. The series recognised the best local open-wheel driver after a hard-fought, year-long battle. Lex Davison won the inaugural title in 1957. Jack was overseas by then, so he'd never been a contender. But in 1987 CAMS converted the series, for one time only, to a one-off event, the Australia Cup. It was a great way to showcase local talent on the weekend of the Australian F1 Grand Prix.

David Brabham qualified last of 27 cars for the fifteen-lap (57-kilometre) race. On the grid, Jack decided to give his youngest son some advice. 'Dad and I had a massive bust-up,' David said. 'I yelled at him to fuck off.' And then David, more steamed up than he'd ever been, drove in anger and frustration through the entire field. Jack was in the pits with his Formula One cronies, proudly pointing out his boy. David took the trophy, an unexpected addition to his CV, and headed for the UK.

The youngest Brabham was the only brother to start motor racing in a go-kart. 'I'd been working on the farm, doing a wool-classing degree because Dad didn't want to pay for a wool classer,' he said. A neighbour got him into karting. He was about to head off to his first race when Jack knocked on the window of the ute: 'I suppose I'd better come with you.' David raced hard in both wet and dry conditions. Jack said: 'The kid can drive.' Within two years, with the help of Jack Brabham Racing and his godfather Ron Tauranac, he'd won the British Formula Three Championship.

Of the three Brabham boys, David was the F1 achiever, even if the car, the Brabham, was, frankly, a dog. David raced the Japanese-owned lame duck Brabham BT59 fourteen times in the 1990 Formula One world championship, failed to qualify six times and failed to finish seven. On the one occasion he saw the chequered flag, in the French Grand Prix, he was fifteenth. And then they wanted him to find $3 million to secure his seat for the 1991 season. He declined.

David Brabham was hired by the Japanese owners of Brabham F1 to bring the 'Brabham lustre' to their BT59 in the 1990 world championship. The car's performance disappointed the entire family.

Four years after the Brabham BT59 attempt, Jack (right) invested in a start-up F1 team, Simtek, with David (left) as its lead driver. Part-owned by technical director Nick Wirth (centre), the Ford-powered S941 did not score a point in the 1994 World Constructors' Championship, and withdrew from the title midway through the 1995 season.

In 1994 he made a second Formula One attempt. The car was called a Simtek and Jack Brabham became a shareholder in the company. It was the love child of then-FIA president Max Mosley and talented race engineer Nick Wirth. Roland Ratzenberger, a 33-year-old rookie, arrived with substantial funding from wealthy Monaco sports management specialist Barbara Behlau. 'She'd taken a shine to him,' Wirth explained, and Ratzenberger took the second car.

In the first two championship rounds, David and Roland scored a twelfth and eleventh each. The third round was the San Marino Grand Prix outside Imola, east of Bologna. The car was tardy coming up to speed: 'Roland struggled, complaining about his brakes,' David recalled. 'The team asked me to try his car. I did for two laps and told them the brakes were shit. They replaced them, and in qualifying I guess he wanted to show everyone how quick he really could be.

'He went off the track, then came straight back on again [without stopping for a check]. The data shows he started weaving from side to side down the straight, then the front wing collapsed at 300 km/h [as a result of the off] and it killed him. I came down the straight and I knew he was dead, the way his neck was. There's a soul in everyone and when it departs, there's nothing.'

It was the first death in a grand prix in twelve years. People had become unaccustomed to it.

Lisa, David's wife, was at the track, pregnant with their son Sam. There was a convention in Formula One that, when there's a fatality, the team withdraws. 'I discussed it with Lisa and with Max and Nick,' David said. 'They said: "It's your decision to race." My brain was fried. Nick said, "If I can reinforce the front wing, see how you feel then."'

Max Mosley (left), FIA president, oversees the Simtek, of which he was part-owner, at the 1994 San Marino Grand Prix. It was a black weekend for motor racing. David Brabham's Simtek teammate Roland Ratzenberger was killed in practice; then former world champion Ayrton Senna died in the race. The fatalities set Mosley on the path of a complete revision of motor-racing safety standards.

David went back out: 'I was experiencing adrenaline like never before. My right leg was moving up and down—I had no control over it. But I ended up quite quick, for us at least. You could sense a dark, dark cloud had lifted. I did the race.'

The next day, three-time world champion Ayrton Senna died on lap seven; vision of his crash was seen in real time around the world. David Brabham, who'd started from the last row of the grid, spun out on lap 27 of the restart. The San Marino Grand Prix entered history as Formula One's darkest day, at least in recent memory.

David raced on with Simtek, but retirements (nine) outweighed finishes (five) and his best result was a tenth. Two of his three teammates hired across the course of the remainder of the season crashed.

There was no farm to return to—Jack had sold that after the last son had left. Not that it was a consideration for David: 'I was very much a racing driver. I never had a thought to retire.' His Formula One career was over but from its ashes came another strong opportunity.

David won the Le Mans 24 Hour, twice in class for Aston Martin, and then outright for Peugeot in 2009. He won the Bathurst 1000 with brother Geoffrey in a 2-litre BMW saloon car ('It was quite a culture shock after F1'). He raced in world sports cars, GT cars, and the American Le Man Series.

It was in 2009 that David became aware that his family's name was in jeopardy. The Brabham 'brand' was being traded among opportunists. A German operator intended entering the 2010 F1 season under the name of Brabham Grand Prix. Another was marketing cars in Europe under the Brabham name. David began a three-year battle in the German courts. Initially Jack joined him, but a separate High Court tussle in Australia over another company using his name and expertise was seizing his attention. At 83, Jack only had the will to take on one fight at a time.

'It cost me everything, every penny,' David claimed. 'I was down to my last £300 [A$450] in the bank. But I won the case. Dad rang me with congratulations, and he sent me some money to keep me going. To me, the Brabham name is iconic. It's up there with Ferrari and McLaren.'

David found partners to help build the icon into a brand. In Adelaide he became involved with the construction of a sleek, swift two-seater sports racing car. The Brabham BT62 broke cover at Mount Panorama in January 2019. I wrote at the time: 'Late in the afternoon, when all was still and the spectators had moved away from the fences, it set a lap time beneath the magic 2-minute mark. It arrived in a rush at the top of the mountain, green and gold, Australia's colours, Jack's colours, and its howl was unworldly. This was the car that David built in

In honour of his father, David Brabham designed and built a limited-edition sports car—the Brabham BT62. It broke cover in Australia at the 2019 Bathurst 12 Hour and set sub-2-minute laps of the 6.213-kilometre Mount Panorama circuit. It was intended that the first 35 produced would each carry the livery of one of Sir Jack's 35 grand prix cars.

Jack's name and it stood for everything that was important in motor racing'—and presumably everything that mattered to the Brabham dynasty.

In 2021 Repco secured naming-rights sponsorship of the Australian Supercars Championship. The opening round was at Mount Panorama, Bathurst, and the company secured Sam Brabham, in Australia seeking his motor-racing fortune, to drive his grandfather's 1966 world championship–winning BT19 Repco Brabham on a tribute lap. David and Lisa watched from lockdown in Great Britain, proud as could be.

6

CURLY AND HAWKEYE
Frank Gardner
Paul Hawkins

ON 30 MAY 1965, PAUL HAWKINS, SON OF A TASMANIAN minister of religion, plunged his Formula One car into the harbour at Monaco.

The car—a British racing-green Lotus 33 Climax previously driven by Jim Clark—sank 10 metres with 28-year-old Hawkins still on board. Only when it settled on the bottom and rescue divers arrived did Hawkins extricate himself, take a huge gulp of air from a proffered mouthpiece and rocket back up to the surface. He'd had the extraordinary presence of mind to hit the engine kill switch just as the car entered the water, saving the very expensive motor owned by a very poor team from instant destruction. It was dried out and used again in the following grand prix.

'It just turned out to sea' was Hawkins' explanation of what had happened. The laconic Hawkins was equalled in his one-line responses only by Sydney's Frank Gardner. The pair were teammates over two years in the European junior categories, enjoying for a time an uproarious rivalry. But in the crucible of world championship grand prix competition, the friendship disintegrated.

Bravery on show: Frank Gardner in the Brabham-BRM gets all four wheels airborne over the Nürburgring's Flugplatz in the 1965 German Grand Prix. Gardner qualified eighteenth, two ahead of Paul Hawkins, but retired on lap one when his gearbox broke.

Gardner drove in nine Formula One world championship races over three seasons. His best result was an eighth. Hawkins participated in just three grands prix in one season and claimed a ninth on debut. But both drivers extensively and successfully raced in other open-wheeler categories as well as in sports and touring cars. They were rough diamond all-rounders—and they revelled in the image.

'I was a good driver, but I wasn't going to be world champion,' the pragmatic Gardner once told me, with unexpected introspection when he returned to Australia after twenty years in Europe. 'It was a different level. I'd follow blokes like Jim Clark, and I'd be doing my very best and they'd be taking an inch here and an inch there. The thing is, Clark couldn't work it out either—he thought everyone should be on his pace. So, I looked elsewhere.'

Gardner won three British Touring Car Championships and the European F5000 title for V8 open-wheeler racing cars. Hawkins died in the attempt. His bright-red Lola T70 GT hit a tree at Oulton Park in the 1969 RAC Tourist Trophy race. He was trapped and incinerated.

Opposite: Bottom of the harbour: Paul Hawkins plunges off the track and into the Monte Carlo yacht basin in the 1965 Monaco Grand Prix. The crash was later replicated by director John Frankenheimer for his seminal film *Grand Prix* (1966).

Above: Frank Gardner, perhaps even a better engineer than he was a driver, strongly influenced the development of formula cars in the UK—from the earliest Brabhams through to a string of Eric Broadley-designed Lolas—then brought his talent back to Australia to design and build championship-winning sports sedans.

'I never wanted to be the world's fastest racing driver,' Gardner quipped. 'I just wanted to be the oldest.'

Gardner—'Curly', because of his increasingly bald head hidden beneath the white terry towelling hat that became his trademark—arrived in England before Hawkins, in 1958. He became Brabham's first works driver, assembling and then racing the Formula Junior cars that gave MRD its baseline. He claimed to have

Paul 'Hawkeye' Hawkins, pockmarked and profane, was a natural racer, inclined to drive around a problem. He was nonetheless a proficient mechanic—a necessary skill in maintaining his own team at a time when multitasking was essential for survival.

built the very first BT2 Brabham Junior from Ron Tauranac's drawings and to have 'locked him out of the workshop while I cut out a few tubes to make it fit'. It was an unlikely story—Tauranac would never have worn a lock-out—but Gardner's recollections, like those of Hawkins, were always spun for colour as much as accuracy.

Gardner learned his craft in Australia. He grew up on Sydney's Northern Beaches as the ward of his uncle Hope Bartlett, one of the heroes of the steeply banked Olympia Motor Speedway at Maroubra. Bartlett helped him prepare his first race cars—Jaguar C- and D-types, both rebuilt from insurance write-offs. He was a natural sportsman—captain of the Whale Beach Surf Life Saving Club, sweep of their surf boat, a low-handicap golfer. Motor racing was his chosen sport and he studied mechanical engineering to understand how race cars worked.

Hawkins—'Hawkeye' (originally 'Hawks', but it grew), six years younger than Gardner— left for England in 1960. He was a wild man. Profanity was his mother tongue; English was his second language. His mother died when he was seven; his father became a minister within the strict discipline of the Apostolic Church. Hawkins bailed as soon as he could—becoming a heavy drinker, smoker and habitual user of swear words that were seldom heard in the fifties. Incredibly, he drank to excess throughout his motor-racing career.

Hawkins talked himself into race drives, even while in his teens. He raced an Austin-Healey 100S, one of the very few brought to Australia, and even drove it in the support race to the 1956 Australian Grand Prix at Albert Park. He learned his hell-raising from the best—John Roxburgh, 'Rocker-Box', later to become the controversial president of CAMS, encouraged mayhem and indulged in a bit himself. Hawkins was caught driving Roxburgh's Cooper Climax at speed on

Melbourne's roads. Rocker-Box didn't mind, but Hawkins, facing serious sanction for other road crimes, shipped out to England.

Gardner went to work for Aston Martin as a race mechanic (he helped them win Le Mans in 1959), then moved on to the Jim Russell Racing Driver School, the training ground for young hopefuls, where he traded mechanical expertise for driving experience.

Hawkins joined Donald Healey's Speed Equipment Division (Austin made Austin-Healeys under licence to Donald) and when works manager John Sprinzel bought the business, Hawkins took over the workshop and some of the driving roles in small-capacity Sprite sports cars—plus the occasional fire-breathing Healey 3000. It was close to a partnership, without money changing hands, and the outgoing Hawkins, full of risqué personality, looked after the company's high-performance customers.

Gardner was just five years younger than Jack Brabham, but Brabham had packed a lot into that half decade—two world titles, for a start. Gardner was the next generation. His role as works driver was little more than Brabham and Ron Tauranac giving him workshop space to build the cars he raced. It didn't come with a lot of money or a partnership. In 1963, when Brabham offered him another year of the same, Gardner thought it prudent to look around first.

Paul Hawkins was the 'pro' in John Sprinzel's 'pro-am' teams. He got to race and party around the world with wealthy amateurs—at Sebring, Le Mans, Monza. In 1962, businessman-club racer Ian Walker formed his own team and took Hawkins with him. Walker was a chum of Colin Chapman, the founder of Lotus. The ebullient Walker—a former Lancaster Bomber tail gunner in World War II, nicknamed 'Walker the Talker' by Chapman—was instrumental in achieving Team Lotus's first major cigarette company sponsorship. The Walker team went fully Lotus—the Type 22 open-wheeler and the Type 23 sports car. It was a step up from Sprinzel's Sprites: a full-blown works team, and a Lotus satellite. Hawkins was racing and winning. When the team expanded the next season, it was Hawkins who suggested Gardner as an addition. The offer involved money and Jack Brabham was disinclined to match it. Jack had another hopeful in the wings anyway—Denny Hulme.

Walker agreed to buy Brabham open-wheelers for the upcoming season. And he couldn't have hoped for more—two hard-as-nails drivers, but they were racing against each other. 'To finish first, first you have to beat your teammate' might look good on paper but in practice it can be mighty expensive. Teams then, as now, needed to manage their drivers.

Gardner was the master of mind games—and he had Hawkins' measure. In the workshop he'd set the engineering standards, while Hawkins, according to Gardner, was 'the willing lad to do the gofer bits'. Hawkins was becoming increasingly frustrated. At Montlhéry in France, Gardner said, 'Paul passed me under brakes, backwards, and put the car into the wall.' They had been running 1–2 at the time. Walker chastised them both.

But they couldn't bring their rivalry in check. As Hawkins became more proficient, Gardner became even less willing to yield. Walker Racing had given them a launch pad and they were in increasing demand. They had become mercenaries, neither suited to the full-time demands of a works team—nor seeking it—but mighty handy to have when grit and determination were needed. Gardner drove for Ford at Le Mans. Hawkins won for Porsche in the Targa Florio. Both would choose to run their own shows. It suited them better.

In 1965 they came together again in a Formula One Team. John Willment Racing, Ford's back-door race team, hired them to race in the Formula One world championship in South Africa. Willment had run Gardner in the 1964 British Saloon Car Championship in a Lotus Cortina, where he'd come eleventh. He'd fielded Hawkins in everything from an AC Cobra to Lotus 23 sports cars.

Hawkins had become something of a South African specialist. He loved the place. The social scene appealed to his single lifestyle, but it suited Gardner less: he was soon to meet Sydney model Gloria Hyde, 'on the sand at Whale Beach, me in the briefest of bikinis,' Gloria recalled with wistful amusement. Two children and a 41-year marriage would follow.

Willment committed to South Africa for the summer season, culminating in the world championship grand prix. Hawkins stayed for it all—his holiday highlights included pouring beer over the head of the mayor of Bulawayo at a prize-giving ceremony, and much, much more. Gardner flew in and out for the races.

In the non-championship Rand Grand Prix in late 1964, Willment hired world champion Graham Hill to race its new V8 Brabham-BRM and Hawkins to drive the team's four-cylinder Brabham BT10 F2 car. Hill won over two heats. Hawkins, fast improving, was second.

The 1965 grand prix season started in South Africa on New Year's Day. Hill, a works driver for BRM, was unavailable. But instead of promoting Hawkins to the V8, Willment brought in Gardner, leaving Hawkins in the four. It was tantamount to incitement. Their antagonism made team life uncomfortable. It would be Hawkins' world championship debut. Gardner had been taken out in a start line crash in the 1964 British Grand Prix at Brands Hatch so if he got off the line, this would be his first world championship race too.

Frank and Gloria Gardner met on Sydney's Whale Beach, where Frank was captain of the surf life saving club. Gloria was a Sydney model who, after Frank's death in 2009, embarked on European sightseeing tours to 'visit all the places I didn't see when we were only going to racetracks'.

Just twenty cars could take the grid on the 3.9-kilometre Prince George Circuit in East London, on the South African coast. Thirty-five turned up to qualify. The top works cars were automatically in; so was Gardner's V8. But Hawkins had to set a time better than 1 minute 37 seconds—quick for a 1500cc Formula Two car. Hawkins hatched a plan. He approached Jack Brabham and asked for a tow. For three laps Brabham was the pathfinder, like a cyclist in a peloton, creating a draft that sucked the slower car along. Brabham qualified at 1 minute 28 seconds, third-fastest on the grid; 1 minute 37 seconds was a small step for him but a giant leap for Hawkins. Brabham towed Hawkins to a time of 1 minute 33 seconds—fastest of all the fifteen pre-qualifiers and, importantly, just behind Gardner. They started fifteenth and sixteenth, Hawkins harrying Gardner. On lap 60 of 85, Gardner's car broke an alternator belt and a lengthy stop dropped him to twelfth. Hawkins sailed past to claim ninth, one place behind Jack Brabham. But Hawkins, miffed by his treatment, left the team anyway.

He did his next deal in a game park, surrounded by elephants. Wealthy privateer Dickie Stoop, a racer of GT cars, would buy the ex-Jim Clark Lotus 33 and they'd take it to Monaco. Of a grid of just seventeen cars, Hawkins qualified fourteenth, Gardner eleventh. Hawkins was challenging for ninth when he headed for the harbour on lap 79 of 100. Ten years before, two-time world champion Alberto Ascari had plunged his Lancia D50 off the pier at the chicane; now it was Hawkins' turn, trailing an advertising banner behind him, like a big canvas sea anchor.

The impetuous Hawkins could be his own worst enemy. He failed to start in the British Grand Prix because he'd gone AWOL, forcing mechanics to test the repaired car themselves—and they crashed it. Frank Gardner came eighth. They faced each other one more time. In the German Grand Prix at the Nürburgring, Gardner qualified eighteenth, Hawkins twentieth. But Gardner's gearbox broke on the first lap; Hawkins' Lotus bottomed out, lost its coolant and stopped on lap three. Stranded, it became a spare parts repository. Dan Gurney and Chris Amon both robbed it of parts for their limping cars. Those things happened in the 1960s.

Opposite: So close. Racing was desperate in the formative classes: in the 1965 Reims Formula Two race, Frank Gardner (Lola T60, right) was narrowly beaten by Jochen Rindt (Brabham BT16, centre) with Jim Clark (Lotus 35, left), third. Just 0.3 seconds separated the three of them. Only Gardner did not become a world champion. Rindt and Clark both died in race crashes.

Above: Paul Hawkins in the ex-Clark Lotus 33 leads Lorenzo Bandini (Ferrari F1512) up the hill at Monaco in 1965 (before Hawkins took his harbour plunge). Bandini finished second to Graham Hill, and died in the same race two years later. Both Bandini and Hawkins won Sicily's Targa Florio sports-car race—Bandini in 1965 in a Ferrari 275 P2, and Hawkins in 1967 in a Porsche 910.

'It's difficult to say why neither of them secured a full-time Formula One drive—they were both as good as Denny Hulme,' claimed David Hobbs, another racer who should have advanced to a works seat. Hobbs is in the unique position of having co-driven with both racers for big wins—with Gardner at the 1962 Le Mans 24 Hour in a Lotus Elite to win the Index of Thermal Efficiency, and eighth outright; and with Hawkins in a Ford GT40 to win the 1000 Kilometres of Monza in 1968, part of the World Sportscar Championship.

'I'd never met Frank before Le Mans,' Hobbs said from his home in Florida. 'He was a lot older than me [eight years]. He was a lot more serious about his racing than Paul. We raced against each other in touring cars and Formula 5000, and he was someone you'd respect mightily. He could drive anything.'

But: 'Paul and I hit it off from the start. He liked a party and so did I. I must admit he led me astray. We found a bar the night before the Daytona 24 Hour and we both started the race with hangovers.' Unprofessional? 'When I look back, it was very unwise, but at the time Mike Hailwood'—nine-time world motorcycle champion—'could stay up all night, drinking and other things, and could still win the Isle of Man TT the next day. I guess it's just different strokes for different folks. Imagine Max Verstappen doing that today. He'd die before he'd allow himself a drink.'

Hobbs regards himself and the two Australians as journeymen. 'I wanted to race for Lotus in the worst possible way, but Colin Chapman had a set against me,' he said. And it comes down to that: motive and opportunity. Getting into the main game was as much about good fortune as skill.

Neither Hawkins nor Gardner got the F1 breaks.

Hobbs recalls testing the works Ford GT40 the night before the 1968 Le Mans 24 Hour race, searching for a mystery vibration. 'I was sitting on the floor—Paul was driving at 280 km/h down a French lane outside the circuit and we figured it was good enough.' It wasn't. In the race, the clutch broke, then the engine blew. 'If he'd been Gardner, we would have insisted on an engine change that night, just to be sure. I guess Frank was the one I'd prefer as a race partner. He was a thinking racer; Paul was balls out.'

On 26 May 1969, Hobbs was sitting on the grid for a round of the European F5000 Championship at Mallory Park when John Webb, owner of Brands Hatch, sought him out. 'John Webb hobbled up to me on his gammy leg and gruffly said: "Your mate—Hawkins—just been killed at Oulton Park—into a tree." Then they dropped the flag.' Hobbs brought his Surtees home second.

Frank Gardner 'boxed on' for another eight years then returned to Australia with his young family, won the Australian Sports Sedan Championship in a car of his own design, and ran the works BMW team in touring-car racing. David Hobbs drove for him in two Bathurst 1000s.

Paul Hawkins (Lola T70, centre) in the BOAC 500 at Brands Hatch, April 1969, which he failed to finish when his rear suspension broke. A month later, in the RAC Tourist Trophy at Oulton Park, Hawkins died in the in the intense blaze of his Lola. The cause of his crash was never determined, although most suspected suspension failure.

For years, Gardner drove the first intervention vehicle in the Australian Grand Prix, sitting alongside his close friend Professor Sid Watkins, the father of motor-racing sports medicine. They were on the scene when two-time world champion Mika Häkkinen crashed at Adelaide in 1995.

'The guy was dead,' Gardner said incredulously. 'But they punched a hole in his throat and jump-started him.' He counted himself fortunate that his own career had been largely incident free. But ulcers developed on his legs, a result of serious cockpit burns during his racing career, and ultimately the struggle to contain them became too much.

Frank Gardner died on 29 August 2009.

7

THE BRUCE AND DENNY SHOW
Bruce McLaren
Denny Hulme

WHAT IF . . .

More than half a century on, the question is relevant even now. What would motor racing, the McLaren team and the world of high-performance road cars look like if Bruce McLaren had survived his testing accident at Goodwood on 2 June 1970?

McLaren is Formula One's second-oldest active team, the second-highest winner of World Drivers' Championship titles (twelve) and the third-highest winner of World Constructors' Championship titles (eight). By the end of 2020 it had achieved 182 grands prix victories. Bruce McLaren had scored its first. Its high-performance road car division produced 4662 cars in 2019, before the impact of the COVID-19 pandemic, and that's about half the total output of Ferrari, with which it has become a lively and legitimate rival.

Bruce's dream—to produce cars woosh-bonk ('woosh'—the suspension goes on; 'bonk'—on goes the body) and win races with them—has long since been surpassed. The McLaren Group has become a corporation.

If you're going to leave a legacy, this is a pretty good one.

In 1968, Bruce McLaren claimed the first world championship grand prix victory for his McLaren team, driving his M7A Ford Cosworth. He took over the lead of the Belgian Grand Prix at Spa-Francorchamps on the last lap when Jackie Stewart was forced to stop for fuel.

Bruce McLaren became the third person, after Brabham and Dan Gurney, to win a grand prix in a car of his own design. It was also McLaren's final grand prix victory, although he came third in the 1969 world championship with a string of high placings.

Bruce McLaren was just 32 when he was killed. He had achieved extraordinary results, as a driver and constructor, in a short space of time. Such a young company could have died with its creator. But Bruce's greatest contribution had not been his driving skill nor his engineering prowess. It had been his humanity. He had built a team of which contemporary HR managers can only dream.

On the afternoon of Bruce's death, his lifelong friend and managing director, fellow New Zealander Phil Kerr, in shock, called the employees together, broke the news and told them to go home and not come in the next day. They should take a day to grieve, he said. (That was the extent of counselling in the 1970s.) But the next morning, everyone turned up for work. There were race cars to be prepared. It was their tribute to Bruce.

A fortnight later, two McLaren M8D sports cars won the first round of the 1970 US Can-Am (for Canadian-American) series, one driven by Denny Hulme, Bruce's loyal number two, the other by American superstar Dan Gurney, who volunteered to temporarily fill the void.

All three had been teammates of Jack Brabham. Two—McLaren and Hulme— had been protégés. Driving as Brabham's Cooper teammate, McLaren had become the youngest ever winner of a world championship grand prix in 1959, aged 22 years and 104 days—a record that would not be broken until 2003. Hulme had won the world championship outright in 1967 when Brabham declined to restrain him with team orders. Once more, Brabham's influence was all over anything good that came from Down Under.

'Jack called our parents his New Zealand Mum and Dad,' Bruce's sister Jan said in the upstairs trophy room of the Bruce McLaren Foundation, a shrine to her brother in an industrial factory unit at Auckland's Hampton Downs race-track. 'Jack used to service his race cars at their garage when he was over for our open-wheeler events.' Brabham was eleven years older than Bruce.

'He'd stay at our home and he was like a big brother. He'd turn up with plastic spiders to frighten the girls and he'd put bungers up the exhaust pipes of cars.' Bruce had led a physically troubled childhood, hampered by a debilitating

condition called Perthes disease, which kept him in and out of traction for three years, and made his left leg four centimetres shorter than the right.

He was prevented from playing contact sports—so motor racing, his dad's passion, was his outlet. Les McLaren—'Pop' to all who knew him—raced a cut-down Austin 7 Ulster and when Bruce was still a wee lad, he got to share it.

The lessons Bruce learned from Jack were invaluable. On top of his own talent, they made him a star. In 1958, out for the New Zealand Grand Prix, Brabham arrived at the McLarens' Remuera garage with two Cooper Climaxes, one for Bruce. 'Pop' bought it. Brabham won the grand prix; Bruce retired with gearbox problems, but he'd done well. By season's end, twenty-year-old Bruce had finished second in the New Zealand Gold Star championship and won the country's inaugural Driver to Europe scholarship, which guaranteed him a Formula Two start with a works team. Jack made sure it was Cooper. Bruce took his special orthopaedic clutch and brake pedals with him.

Opposite: From 1967, Bruce McLaren's sports cars dominated the North American Can-Am series. The distinctive papaya McLarens, ranging from the M6A (1967) to the M8F (1971), delivered five successive series wins—two each to Bruce McLaren and Denny Hulme, and the final one to Peter Revson.

Above: No doubt about it: Bruce McLaren (left) owed a lot to Jack Brabham. Bruce won New Zealand's Driver to Europe scholarship, but it was Brabham who cleared the path to the youngster becoming his number two at Cooper in his first grand prix season. Bruce called Jack his godfather. On the flight back to England from the 1970 Indianapolis 500, Bruce told Jack he was planning to retire and just go testing. 'But that's the most dangerous thing we do,' Jack responded.

His first world championship grand prix, a one-off, was in Germany, on the Nürburgring's 22.8-kilometre Nordschleife circuit, and in a Formula Two Cooper he came a sensational fifth outright. It was the race in which Englishman Peter Collins was flung from his works Ferrari and died.

In 1959, Cooper promoted Bruce McLaren to its Formula One team, number two to Brabham in the year Jack won his first world championship. McLaren claimed sixth in the title, elevated four positions by his spectacular win in the final-round US Grand Prix at Sebring—the race in which he became the youngest driver to win a world championship Formula One grand prix.

Jack and Bruce dominated the New Zealand Grand Prix in early January 1960. Jack won, with Bruce just 0.6 seconds behind, and in tenth place was Denny Hulme, still at home in New Zealand and already pushing 25.

Denny Hulme won his world F1 title with Jack Brabham in 1967, and the Can-Am series with Bruce McLaren in 1968 and for McLaren in 1970. Without ambition to own his own team, 'The Bear' was regarded by both Brabham and McLaren as the best and most loyal number two they could possibly hire.

In seniority, Denny should have been New Zealand's first Driver to Europe, but Bruce had enjoyed a dream run. Denny's path had been rocky. He was a barefoot lad from the back blocks—not because of poverty but because that's what you did in 'Footrot Flats'. Denny's non-shoe-wearing habit extended to the workshop and to his race car—he said it gave him more feel. Then he dropped an engine block on his unprotected toes in Brabham's UK shop. That changed his tune.

The Hulmes lived on a farm at Pongakawa on the Bay of Plenty. Denny's dad Clive, a World War II hero and winner of the Victoria Cross—the Commonwealth's greatest military recognition for bravery—practised tough love. There wasn't a lot of personal encouragement, but Clive surprised a teenaged Denny when he bought him an MGA, the very latest in sports-car technology. He converted that into race wins and traded up to a Cooper.

It won him the next Driver to Europe scholarship. Denny shared the prize with George Lawton, son of the local mayor. They formed the unofficial 'New Zealand International Grand Prix Team' and split costs racing Formula Two wherever they could in the UK and on the continent. As 'teammates' they agreed to be gentlemen, play nicely, right up to the time a paid or free drive emerged. Then it was every man for himself.

Jack and Bruce blitzed Formula One in 1960. Jack won his second world title. Bruce won the first round in Argentina and came second in the championship overall. Jack also won the Formula Two world championship. They raced as much as they could. Promoters paid good starting money and even the works teams needed the cash. Jack towed his works car up to Copenhagen for the non-championship Danish Grand Prix on the tiny Roskilde Ring. Denny and George Lawton went too. The 1.19-kilometre track offered no relief. There were no straights and no safety fences. The lap record was just 43.2 seconds. Brabham won the race, but Lawton was killed. He clipped an inside verge on a fast left-hander and the Cooper pirouetted, flinging its unbelted driver out. Denny cradled his friend as he died.

Lawton had secured a non-championship Formula One drive in the Lombank Trophy at Snetterton the following weekend. It would have been a real career breakthrough. The Yeoman Credit Racing team offered the seat to Hulme and he came fifth in a F1 Cooper Climax, one lap behind Team Lotus's Innes Ireland and Jim Clark.

There was a gulf between McLaren and Hulme. Bruce was on top of his game; Denny was struggling just to feed himself. So Bruce stepped in to help. He loaned Denny his Morris Minor, the car he'd bought for a peppercorn from

Betty Brabham. Bruce was doing so well that he'd become the proud owner of one of the first E-type Jaguars; the car companies liked to look after F1 stars. Bruce's friend Phil Kerr, then working for Brabham, arranged for Denny to be employed by Jack Brabham Motors—Jack's general garage and filling station in suburban Chessington, on the edge of Greater London. Kerr kept pushing Hulme's case to Brabham, and when Frank Gardner left Brabham's Motor Racing Developments (MRD) to join Ian Walker, Denny got a look-in. Jack gave him a one-off drive in the Formula Junior car, just to see how he'd go. He put the car on pole at Crystal Palace and finished fourth with mechanical gremlins. Then, with Jack's growing approval, he went to the Brands Hatch Boxing Day meeting, won, and set a lap record.

Denny Hulme had become part of Jack Brabham's circle of trust, a works driver in the lower formulae for the 1963 season with a space in the corner to build his own car.

In 1962, when Brabham left Cooper, Bruce McLaren was promoted to the team's number-one position. He repaid them by winning the Monaco Grand Prix by just 1.3 seconds from world champion Phil Hill in the shark-nose Ferrari that had dominated the first season of the new 1.5-litre F1. And he brought the Cooper home third in the world title behind Graham Hill (BRM) and Jim Clark (Lotus). Bruce was the second of five drivers from Australasia to win the blue-riband Monaco race, a remarkable Down Under record.

Being at Cooper without Brabham was hard for Bruce McLaren. Charlie Cooper felt betrayed by Brabham's departure and would not let McLaren near his designs for fear he'd steal them, just as he believed Jack had. When McLaren asked to take two Coopers to Australia and New Zealand for the inaugural Tasman Series, Charlie Cooper declined. And that forced the issue. Bruce registered Bruce McLaren Motor Racing Limited, modified the cars and took them himself.

The money for the effort came from a wealthy Pennsylvania family, the Mayers. Timmy Mayer, 26, was the driver along with Bruce; Teddy, his elder brother, was the tax lawyer–brains of the outfit. Timmy was keen to drive in the 1964 F1 season. The Tasman Series would be an ideal showcase.

Timmy was a runaway success: third in the New Zealand Grand Prix, fourth in the Australian Grand Prix. He was star material, handsome, charming, and he was on target to claim third in the championship behind Bruce and Jack Brabham. But at the last round, at Longford—the 7.2-kilometre temporary circuit outside Launceston that ultimately claimed a lap record average of 196.62 km/h, then the fastest in Australia—Timmy crashed in practice and was killed.

When Jack Brabham left Cooper to begin Motor Racing Developments (MRD), Bruce McLaren took over the number-one Cooper spot. Here, at the Monaco Grand Prix in 1965, Jack Brabham (Brabham Climax) leads Bruce McLaren (Cooper Climax). Brabham retired with engine failure and McLaren came fifth.

Bruce McLaren came second in the race the next day, enough to clinch the Tasman Series championship. Teddy Mayer went home to the United States to contemplate the morality of a sport that built fast cars in which young men killed themselves, then returned to the UK and encouraged Bruce to go out on his own. They became 50:50 partners in McLaren Racing.

Bruce saw out his contract with Cooper, finished seventh in the 1964 championship and eighth in the 1965 title and began beavering away at his own future.

Denny Hulme became a works Formula One driver in 1965. He alternated with Jack Brabham and Dan Gurney in MRD's 1.5-litre Brabham to claim eleventh in the title. Then Gurney left to start his own team, All American Racers. Brabham had not been certain Hulme was Formula One material but, without Gurney, he was prepared to elevate him to full status in 1966—the first year of the 3-litre formula in which he would debut his Australian Repco V8.

Brabham's championship win made history. Hulme loyally followed him home in fourth, the pair collecting the necessary points to claim the World Constructors' Championship title. Bruce McLaren, dipping a toe in the water with his own team, entered five world title grands prix that year and came home fourteenth.

Halfway through the year, Bruce and Denny had been brought together for the first time by American Carroll Shelby. They'd contested the Le Mans 24 Hour in Shelby's works Ford GT40s, the race immortalised in the Hollywood film *Ford v Ferrari*. McLaren and fellow Kiwi Chris Amon won. Denny, with British-American Ken Miles, was second.

Encouraged by Teddy Mayer, Bruce had become obsessed with the lucrative new US Can-Am sports-car championship series, and had run Amon in selected

events in an innovative car, the Zerex Special, originally raced by US motor-racing billionaire Roger Penske. Bruce was keen to make Amon part of his Formula One future too, but Amon was called up by Enzo Ferrari with an offer too good to refuse. So Bruce turned to Denny.

Opposite: The controversial 1-2-3 finish at the 1966 Le Mans 24 Hour race, a victory celebration set up by Ford's PR team, was said to have robbed Ken Miles and Denny Hulme (#1) of victory in favour of Bruce McLaren and Chris Amon (#2). The photo clearly shows McLaren edged to the front at the flag from the Miles/Hulme car. Third-placed Ronnie Bucknum and Dick Hutcherson were two laps down.

Below: When Jack Brabham's suspension broke at 240 km/h in practice for the 1967 German Grand Prix, giving Jack a huge scare, Denny stopped and gave him a lift back to the pits perched on his own car (here at the Nürburgring's Karussell). Jack could have pulled rank and taken over Denny's car. Instead, the pair raced to a 1-2 victory the next day. Hulme won, a big fillip to his world-championship contention.

In 1967, Denny raced for Brabham in Formula One and for McLaren in Can-Am. It was the best year of his life. He won the Formula One world championship; Brabham came second. He came second in the Can-Am championship; McLaren was first. To top it off, Denny won Rookie of the Year in the Indianapolis 500, in Dan Gurney's All American Racers Eagle.

Curiously, Denny had not reached star status—not like Jim Clark, Graham Hill or Jack Brabham. He won the 1967 Monaco Grand Prix, the third of the Down Under contingent to do so, and was greeted by a minder whose job it was to lead the victor up to the podium to meet Prince Rainier and Princess Grace. 'Pardon,' the functionary asked, 'but what is your name?'

Hulme's win in the 1967 world championship was a testament to Jack Brabham's sense of fair play. Going into the last round, the Mexican Grand Prix, Brabham could have still claimed his fourth title if he'd won the race and Hulme had come fourth or lower. It might have been possible to manipulate the result. But Brabham offered no team orders. Jim Clark won, Brabham was second, Hulme third. 'He did the right thing,' Brabham said afterwards. 'He spent the race glued to my tail.' Denny, in Jack's view, had matured into a 'fine driver'.

Bruce McLaren's Speedy Kiwi logo became one of the best known in Formula One. Some thought it was a flying Kiwi—but not even Bruce could achieve that.

Bruce McLaren was the proudest of Kiwis. When he left on the Driver to Europe scholarship, he wore a specially made blazer—black with a silver fern stripe. When he designed his team's logo it was, naturally, a 'speedy kiwi'. And when he hired for his growing team, his distinct preference was for fellow countrymen. In 1968 he poached Denny Hulme from their mutual mentor Jack Brabham. And for good measure he stole Phil Kerr, Brabham's general manager.

The Bruce and Denny Show was born that year.

On 9 June 1968, at Spa-Francorchamps in Belgium, Bruce claimed the first victory for McLaren Formula 1. He stood on the podium, his car alongside BRM and Ferrari. It was his fourth F1 victory—three with Cooper, one with his own team—but tragically it would be his last. Denny put two more wins on the board for McLaren that year too, in Italy and Canada.

For two years—1968 and 1969—the McLaren Formula One team knocked on the door of a world title. Denny was third in the 1968 championship, and Bruce was fifth. The team was tenth in the Constructors' championship. In 1969, Bruce was third;

Live broadcast, 1960s style: Bruce McLaren (McLaren M7B) blasts past a live-to-air studio camera operator en route to fifth place in the 1969 Monaco Grand Prix, one place ahead of Denny Hulme. Ironically, 1969 is hailed as the first year that genuine efforts were made to put circuit safety measures in place.

Denny was sixth, with a win in Mexico. And the team advanced to fourth in the Constructors' championship. They were good and happy times.

In Can-Am racing they swept all before them. The bright yellow (papaya) McLaren sports cars totally dominated the US category. The pair went to the Indianapolis 500 in 1969 to race for Carroll Shelby, who'd masterminded their Le Mans 1–2 back in 1966. They narrowly escaped with their reputations intact— and, they reasoned, their lives. The attempt was funded by McLaren's sponsor Goodyear, and their turbine car, according to a letter Bruce wrote home, was dangerous and built outside the rules. 'Denny and I had to voice our suspicions to Goodyear,' Bruce wrote. 'The next thing we knew the cars had been withdrawn "for reasons of safety" . . . Goodyear just closed the whole operation down and let Shelby make a statement that was acceptable and allowed him to bow out with some good grace.'

Indianapolis remained an itch Bruce and Denny wanted to scratch. Bruce launched a massive assault in 1970, in the month that ended in his death.

McLaren built a special car, the M15, for Denny. Bruce wasn't intending to drive—according to his sister Jan, he was in constant discomfort from his hips, a result of his childhood Perthes disease. He was planning to undergo what was then a radical hip replacement operation, with a surgeon recommended by Jack Brabham, and to retire from active competition.

At Indianapolis, the 'speedy Kiwi' team fielded Chris Amon and Denny Hulme. Amon was the first to falter. One of the bravest men in F1 just couldn't consistently get up to speed against the Brickyard's walls and he withdrew. Then Denny caught fire in practice. At 280 km/h, the fuel filler cap came loose under pressure and sprayed methanol over him and the engine. He washed speed off and bailed out at around 110 km/h. His body was protected by fireproof overalls, but his hands were badly burned as his leather gloves melted into his skin. Bruce hired two American drivers—Peter Revson and Carl Williams—and they salvaged a ninth and 22nd.

The day after Indy, Bruce flew home. He was working at a frenetic pace. He had the Belgian Grand Prix the following weekend, the first round of the Can-Am a week later, and the Dutch Grand Prix a week after that.

It was 2 June 1970. Bruce went to Goodwood, in Sussex, to bed in the F1 and sports cars. The sports car was taking some development. New regulations had required the mounting points of its rear aerodynamic wing to be moved from the suspension to the body. It was a big change.

At 12.19 p.m., Bruce left the pits for a high-speed run. The team heard the big Chev V8 rev out normally, around the back of the flat Goodwood track, and

Denny Hulme returned from the 1970 Indianapolis 500 with both hands bandaged, salving his severe burns. If not for his injuries Hulme would have tested his Can-Am car at Goodwood on 2 June 1970, not Bruce McLaren.

then . . . silence. New Zealand mechanic Jim Stone—later to run Stone Brothers Racing in Supercars in Australia—grabbed a fire extinguisher and rushed to the scene. The wing had let go, the car had turned sharply into an immovable barrier, and Bruce was dead.

'Denny and I had caught the Tube to London that morning to see a specialist about his hands,' Greeta Hulme, Denny's wife, remembered. 'We'd left our son Martin with a neighbour, and when we got there, she said she'd just heard the news—Bruce had been killed.' The Hulmes hurried to Patty McLaren's side; Denny, according to Phil Kerr, was beyond reason. He blamed himself—if not for his burned hands, he would have been testing the car, not Bruce.

COOPER
The Cooper Car Company Ltd.
9 HILL Phil
10 MAC LAREN Bruce

Bruce McLaren met his wife Patty Broad at a Saturday-night dance at Timaru, New Zealand. When he won the Driver to Europe scholarship, Bruce asked her to follow him to the UK. They were married in 1961. Despite his early wins, it took some time for Bruce to become a household name—note the spelling of his name in the 1964 Monaco pits.

But by the next morning, he'd rallied. Denny Hulme, quiet, taciturn in the Jack Brabham mould, rose to a new level of practical leadership. 'Denny anchored the team,' Australian McLaren engineer Steve Roby told me. 'There was always a commitment he'd have a car.' Denny was fourth in the world championship in 1970, the year of Bruce's death. The team faltered in 1971, but in the next three years Denny was third, sixth and seventh, with a grand prix win in each season. He claimed six of his eight grand prix victories with McLaren.

But the team's management was changing and in 1974 Peter Revson, who'd become a close friend of Hulme, was jettisoned, a casualty of politics and sponsorship requirements. Revson found a new seat with the American-owned UOP Shadow F1 team and he crashed in testing at Kyalami in South Africa. There were no medical services readily available. Denny and Graham Hill commandeered a car and sped to the scene, but they could not save him. For the second time in his career, Denny had been with a good friend at the moment of his death.

It was then he decided to retire. He saw out the season and when his engine quit after just four laps at the final-round Watkins Glen US Grand Prix, he quietly walked to the team's helicopter and flew away. A New Zealand or Australian driver would not compete for McLaren again until Daniel Ricciardo joined the team in 2021.

Bruce's 'speedy kiwi' logo was retired in 1981. His daughter Amanda is an ambassador for the modern McLaren car brand in the UK. Denny Hulme died in 1992, aged 56, racing a BMW M3 for Frank Gardner's team in the Bathurst 1000 at Mount Panorama. He suffered a heart attack, and his last act was to pull safely to the side of Conrod Straight.

8

BEST OPPORTUNITY . . . WORST LUCK
Chris Amon
David Walker

'IF CHRIS AMON WAS AN UNDERTAKER, PEOPLE WOULD stop dying,' Mario Andretti, the man whose name is synonymous with speed, said of the New Zealander regarded as the best driver never to win a world championship grand prix. He might well have been talking about Australia's David Walker as well. Walker was not the talent that Amon was—although he was allowed precious little time to develop it—but, like Amon, he earned the right to be a works driver for one of the best teams in the championship.

And it went nowhere for both of them.

Chris Amon spent two and a half seasons with Ferrari's Formula One team—and became its leader after the death of his first teammate Lorenzo Bandini. He remains the only New Zealander or Australian to have been a works Ferrari F1 driver (the distinction is F1—Tim Schenken was a works Ferrari sports-car star). Amon's timing was terrible. He joined the world's most successful team during one of its dysfunctional periods.

David Walker was hired by Colin Chapman's John Player Team Lotus at the height of their powers. His misfortune was that his teammate was Emerson

Chris Amon guides his Ferrari 312 V12 through the forest at Spa-Francorchamps in the 1967 Belgian Grand Prix. He finished third to Dan Gurney (Eagle Weslake) and Jackie Stewart (BRM), with Jochen Rindt (Cooper Maserati, chasing) in fourth. Amon's Ferrari teammate Mike Parkes broke both his legs in a first lap roll-over and never raced world-championship F1 again.

Fittipaldi. He would be saddled with the unenviable reputation of being the only driver to score zero points in the year their teammate won the world championship.

Amon raced in 96 championship grands prix for ten teams across fourteen seasons to claim just eleven podiums and 83 career points. Walker was more succinct—one season, one team, no points.

The statistics are stark, and they underestimate the talent of both drivers. They also expose the ruthless underbelly of F1. There is nowhere to hide, and performance is all that counts.

CHRIS AMON

Chris Amon was sixteen when he started his first proper motor race in his first proper race car in April 1961. It was a 1.5-litre Cooper Climax and he was on the outside of the front row of the grid at the now defunct Levin, a kidney-shaped circuit within a horseracing track, 100 kilometres north of Wellington on New Zealand's North Island. The pole sitter was Duncan McKenzie in the ex-Jack Brabham 2-litre Cooper. Amon was off like a rabbit and headed McKenzie into the first corner. Then the red flag came out and stopped the race. McKenzie had rolled his Cooper in pursuit and was killed, the only fatality in the circuit's twenty-year history. Amon decided a spindly Cooper was not for him and traded it for a more substantial Maserati 250F. Juan Manuel Fangio had used one to win the world title in 1954.

In his sixties, Chris took me to see the car at the Southward Car Museum at Paraparaumu: 'It had so much power,' he said, his eyes alive with teenage excitement. 'You couldn't drive it on brake and steering—it would just plough ahead. You drove it on the throttle. The more you applied the power, the livelier it would get, and you just modulated it.'

Eighteen-year-old Chris drove the 250F to eleventh in the rain-swept 1962 New Zealand Grand Prix on the Ardmore airfield circuit. Stirling Moss won: 'At one stage I got pretty sideways, and Moss lapped me on the inside and gave me a cheery wave—he thought I was moving out of his way.'

Amon once took pains to play down his background of privilege. Later, he didn't care so much. It was hard to avoid the fact that as a fifteen-year-old he'd flown in his instructor's Tiger Moth from his elite boarding college and landed in one of his parents' paddocks for Sunday lunch. Or that when he attracted the attention of Australian team owner David McKay, his family was able to fund the teenager's entry into the world of McKay's Scuderia Veloce. His training car was the Cooper Climax Bruce McLaren had used in 1959 to win his first world championship grand prix at Sebring.

For his entire career, and beyond, Chris Amon (left) was a chain-smoker—even in the pits. The charismatic Amon enjoyed strong support from global media including Mike Kable (right), the founding national motoring editor of *The Australian*.

In 1963, Reg Parnell, British team owner and star-maker, snatched Amon away to race in Europe. There would be no junior categories, no learning curve, and, for that matter, no living rough. Parnell had struck a deal with an oil company to insert Amon straight into Formula One. He would be paid from the outset and he would be replacing seven-time world motorcycle champion John Surtees, who was moving to Ferrari (where he won the 1964 world title). Amon was just nineteen.

He flew out, alone, in April (his first jet flight), raced Parnell's Lola-Climax into fifth place in a non-championship event at Goodwood and then travelled to the first round of the 1963 world championship, which was held in Monaco. There could be no more daunting place to debut, but no more an inspiring place either.

Parnell made his other Lola available to veteran and local hero Maurice Trintignant. Neither car was super-fast, not compared to the Lotus of pole sitter Jim Clark. But when Trintignant did a qualifying lap in 1 minute 41.3 seconds, Amon responded with an impressive 1 minute 41.4 seconds. Then the Frenchman blew his engine and Parnell gave him Amon's car. It was Amon's first taste of F1 reality.

That year Amon scored two consecutive seventh places—one at the high-speed slipstreaming Reims circuit in the French Grand Prix, the next with a new experimental Coventry Climax engine in the British Grand Prix. It had so much power that, with a momentary loss of concentration at Monza in the Italian Grand Prix, he speared off the track and put himself into hospital with broken ribs.

It got worse: enforced confinement turned to deep-vein thrombosis and a two-month lay-off.

And then worse again: Parnell sent one of the Lolas for Amon to race in the first Tasman Series season. It was there he received the horrible news that 52-year-old Parnell had died from peritonitis, the aftermath of an appendix operation. Twenty-year-old Chris Amon believed his career had ended.

Tim Parnell, Reg's son, scrambled to save the team and achieved the seemingly impossible. It was a cart and horse dilemma. In order to retain the team's sponsors, he needed good drivers and in order to secure good drivers, he needed sponsors. He accomplished both. He signed nine-time world motorcycle champion Mike Hailwood, son of a millionaire businessman; aspiring newcomer Peter Revson, part heir to the Revlon fortune; and appointed Amon, perhaps the least well-heeled of the three, as his number one.

The trio shared a first-floor flat in Ditton Road, Surbiton, and became the Ditton Road Flyers, convenors of the best-known party house of the 1960s. 'It was never as wild as legend has it,' Amon told me many years later, but he was grinning broadly when he said it. It's a shame the racing wasn't as good. Chris was sixteenth in the championship with two points; Mike and Peter were equal nineteenth with one.

That was when Bruce McLaren stepped in. He took on the care of young Amon, arranging sports-car drives for him and offering employment in his burgeoning team. McLaren Formula One was always the promise. In 1966, aged just 22, Chris co-drove with Bruce in the winning Ford GT40 at the Le Mans 24 Hour race.

Bruce McLaren raced his Formula One car for the first time in 1966, but there wasn't yet one for the impatient Amon. In late '66 Chris was invited to Maranello to meet Enzo Ferrari. Incredibly, the Commendatore (as Ferrari liked to be known)

Chris Amon believed he had betrayed countryman Bruce McLaren by accepting a works drive with Ferrari. Here his Ferrari passes Bruce McLaren's M7A (#10) in the pits of the 1968 French Grand Prix at Rouen. In qualifying, Amon was sandwiched between the McLarens of Denny Hulme and Bruce McLaren—separated by just 0.3 seconds. The McLarens beat Amon in the race.

had chosen the young New Zealander as his next big chance. This was an offer too good to refuse, but his leaving caused a rift with McLaren.

On 7 May 1967, Chris Amon took to the Formula One grid for the first time with Ferrari, at the Monaco Grand Prix. He was number two to five-year Ferrari veteran Lorenzo Bandini; the pair had already won the Daytona 24 Hour and Monza 1000 together in the 4-litre Ferrari P4, and had become good friends. They had driven to Monaco together, after Amon had waited outside a house in Modena where Bandini 'said goodbye' to his mistress.

On lap 82, Bandini was chasing Denny Hulme in the Brabham for first place when he hit a concealed bollard above the harbour quay chicane and suffered fatal burns. A media helicopter had fanned the fire. Amon came third.

Chris Amon drives away from the flames that fatally engulfed his Ferrari team leader Lorenzo Bandini in the 1967 Monaco Grand Prix. Amon and the rest of the field were forced to drive past the crash site for the remaining eighteen laps of the race. Amon, deeply affected, finished third.

Bandini and Amon had been due to fly that night to the qualifying sessions for the Indianapolis 500. 'I had a lot of time on the plane to think about the what-ifs,' Chris said. He failed to qualify at Indy. 'I actually felt fear.'

Amon was promoted to Ferrari's number one, and he did well. He made four visits to the podium and was fifth in the championship, a good result in a year in which the Brabhams were dominant. In 1968, Ferrari brought in Belgian Jacky Ickx, two years Amon's junior and, in his view, his number two. When Chris learned Ickx was being paid substantially more, he fronted Enzo Ferrari to ask why. 'You never asked for more,' the Commendatore replied, and upped his salary.

The notorious 'Amon curse' that dogged Chris his entire career was on full display in '68. He outqualified Ickx 8:2, but Ickx brought his Ferrari home fourth in the title and Amon was tenth. 'I should have won the championship,' he later lamented. But a stone through his radiator, a broken gearbox when he was comfortably in the lead and a rear-wing collapse at Monza that sent him airborne all worked against him.

Opposite: The Commendatore, Enzo Ferrari (right), seen here with engineeer Mauro Forghieri (centre), had high regard for Chris Amon (left). They spent hours together driving in the hills outside Modena. Ferrari was distressed when Amon quit the team mid-season in 1969.

Above: The Amon AF101 was a disastrous attempt by Amon to build his own F1 car and run his own team. He raced it only once himself in the 1974 Spanish Grand Prix, where he qualified 24th from 26 starters and retired at quarter-distance when the brakes failed.

Amon became so frustrated he quit Ferrari halfway through the 1969 season. He had just turned 26. 'It was a damned silly decision,' he told me many years later. 'The old man [Enzo Ferrari] wanted me to come back, you know.' But he never went.

From then on, he played musical chairs with team changes: first, the promising start-up British-owned March Formula One ('a total con,' he claimed, although he visited the podium three times and finished eighth in the title in 1970); then two years with the French Matra team (he was leading at Monza, when he tried to remove a clear plastic tear-off from his visor, which restores vision, and took off the entire visor instead, blinding himself with a 300 km/h blast of air). He went to another start-up, Tecno, then had a brief two-race interlude with Tyrell that was cut short when his teammate François Cevert was killed in the US Grand Prix at Watkins Glen.

Amon toyed with building his own car, the Amon AF101, but raced it only once in Spain and retired it when its brakes failed. He raced twice for BRM, then joined Mo Nunn's Ensign team for almost two seasons. His results curve was locked in the descendancy.

In 1976, world champion Niki Lauda had his fiery crash at the Nürburgring, his life saved by other drivers who pulled him from the wreck. There was an hour before the race was to resume—time to think. Chris walked up to Mo Nunn and said he was not going to take the restart, bringing his career to a close. In truth, he made a desultory attempt to drive for the Wolf-Williams team in the Canadian Grand Prix at year's end, but he was involved in a warm-up lap T-bone crash and was classified as a non-starter. His bad luck held true, right to the end.

In 1977, Chris and his wife Tish moved to New Zealand, where they raised three children—Georgina, and twin sons Alex and James—on their large dairy farm. Many people who met him in the second half of his life knew him only as a farmer. Enzo Ferrari, who retained affection for him throughout, said in his memoirs: 'I wonder if his children believed him when he told them how very near he had been to becoming a motor-racing legend.'

Chris died in 2016 from cancer. He was 73.

DAVID WALKER

Toxicity killed David Walker's chances of becoming a world champion. From the start of his sole F1 season with John Player Team Lotus, the Sydney-born, King's School–educated racer was at odds with his team principal, Peter Warr. He was fired for breach of contract with three grands prix to go, then reinstated for the last event—which he failed to finish when his engine blew.

Walker had been a rising star in the junior categories. The 21-year-old, driving the very earliest Brabham BT2, was fourth in the inaugural Australian Formula Junior Championship and second in the very first Australian Formula Two Championship. 'I'd been into speed as a kid,' Walker said from his home in the Whitsundays, where he'd run luxury yacht charters through the Great Barrier

David Walker was highly regarded by his peers, including world champion Alan Jones, but his F1 career was cut short by what seemed to be his inability to come to terms with the Lotus 72, perhaps fuelled by a toxic political environment—not the first or last time a driver has been similarly affected.

Reef. His first racing success came in a twin-cam MGA when he won his first hill climb.

In 1962, like Chris Amon, he struck up an association with David McKay's Scuderia Veloce (Amon drove McKay's 2.5-litre Cooper; Walker drove initially in his own Formula Junior Brabham), balanced by sage advice from Geoff Sykes, general secretary of the Australian Automobile Racing Club, which ran Warwick Farm racecourse: 'Get overseas as soon as you can.' The opportunity arose three years later. He crashed his Formula Two Brabham heavily in the 1965 Tasman Series round at Lakeside in Queensland and, without a car, left the country.

He arrived in the UK with £100 [A$183] in his pocket, and with skill and persuasion he talked his way into the use of a British-built Merlyn F3 car. Walker and Swiss-Australian Kurt Keller, who had been his engine tuner in Australia, crisscrossed Europe, sleeping in their transporter, picking up starting money and living off the proceeds. Close to the Iron Curtain, Walker won the 1967 Adriatic Grand Prix on the picturesque Opatija circuit, known as the Monaco of the East in what is now Croatia—and that was enough for Mike Warner, managing director of Lotus Components, Colin Chapman's customer division, to offer him a works drive.

Walker became one of the best of the junior-category drivers. In three years racing for Lotus, he won the Formula Ford and Formula Three championships run by the British Racing and Sports Car Club, along with two parallel British F3 titles. Colin Chapman promoted him straight to Formula One. He did two preliminary races in 1971. 'It was a big jump,' David said with some understatement. 'They put me into the Lotus 56, their turbine car.'

The 56 was one of Chapman's grand experiments. It was all-wheel drive, powered by a Pratt & Whitney jet engine, and Chapman had built the wedge-shaped aerodynamic prototype to see if he could run just one design in both Formula One and IndyCar. Mike Spence had been killed in one at Indianapolis in 1968.

Walker was given the 56B, a wide-body version, necessary to carry sufficient fuel for a grand prix. 'It caught fire at Hockenheim, so we decided it was best not

to race it,' Walker said. It rained during the Dutch Grand Prix and that suited the all-wheel drive: 'I was lapping faster than the leaders.' But the car suffered from unintended acceleration. 'As soon as you came off the brakes it started accelerating again. On lap 22 I parked it in a sandbank.'

In 1972, Chapman entered him in the full world championship, alongside lead driver Emerson Fittipaldi. His season in the purpose-built Lotus 72 should have been sensational. The 72 was a great car. Lotus's posthumous 1970 world

Opposite: Two debutants together. Colin Chapman's ambitious and revolutionary Lotus 56B wedge car, powered by a Pratt & Whitney turbine engine, made its debut in the 1971 Dutch Grand Prix along with its driver, David Walker, a star of the lesser racing categories. Walker did a good job of managing the 'wedge'.

Below: In the 1972 South African Grand Prix, David Walker (Lotus 72), right, puts a passing move on Helmut Marko (BRM), the man who would later have a huge influence on the careers of Mark Webber and Daniel Ricciardo. Walker finished tenth; Marko was fourteenth.

Controversy surrounds Walker's single F1 season in 1972. His team claimed he lacked mechanical sympathy and was physically unfit for the rigours of F1. He counterclaimed that he was excluded from an equal share of testing and was denied mid-season upgrades. He came nowhere near to living up to the potential of a driver regarded as one of the most promising of the junior-category contenders.

champion Jochen Rindt, after securing his first victory in a 72, said that 'a monkey could win in that car'.

Walker thought he had done everything he could to show Lotus he was committed. He had even moved to Norfolk to be close to the factory: 'But Peter Warr was pushing me from the start—even when I signed the contract, he was telling me there were others he could secure; Ronnie Peterson was in his hip pocket, he said.'

History records that Walker was never on Fittipaldi's pace in the Lotus 72—he has to wear the ignominy of scoring no points in his teammate's championship-winning season. And there's no getting around that. Walker claims he received no help. 'I was never comfortable in the car—the gear change was in the wrong place for me. I was never allowed to do a full practice session, never taken to the track in advance to walk the circuit. In Spain, Fittipaldi borrowed my car and buggered the gearbox. I ran out of fuel and Warr gave me a hard time for using too many revs. I learned later that Fittipaldi had a different engine. At the end of the season, I got to drive his car and it was chalk and cheese—his was 1000 rpm up.'

All of which any reasonable person would take with a grain of salt. Racing drivers' excuses have always been a dime a dozen, especially back then when there was no telemetry to disprove them. And yet . . . at the end of 1971, Mike Warner, the man who'd hired Walker to Lotus, had left the company when the customer division closed, and he cherry-picked the best of Lotus's engineers to go with him to a new rival organisation called Group Racing Developments (GRD). There's a strong possibility that Warr felt stuck with Warner's man, who, worse still, was on a three-year contract.

The matter came to a head when three-quarters of the way through the 1972 season Warner invited Walker to test the new GRD Formula Two car. 'I took that request to Warr, who said I could,' Walker swears. 'But afterwards he denied he'd given permission and claimed I was in breach of my contract because I'd tested another car. I didn't have his agreement in writing, nothing to take to Colin Chapman.' And with that he was out.

David Walker had a huge road accident in 1973, badly damaging his left arm: 'I still can't move my thumb, clench a fist, or use a screwdriver or spanner.' Mike Warner gave him a test of the GRD F2 car 'and I would have stayed', but the GRD venture folded from lack of cash. In Canada, Walker put a Formula Atlantic car on pole position at the Shubenacadie circuit in Nova Scotia and a young driver, Gilles Villeneuve, walked up and said, 'Now I know how fast I have to go if I want to be a Formula One driver.'

'It was,' said Walker, 'a lovely compliment.'

David and his Canadian wife Janet began building boats, then sailed one back to the Whitsundays, where life has been idyllic.

Except, half a century on: 'I still lie in bed at night and get angry with Peter Warr.'

9

IN THE SAME POND
Howden Ganley
Tim Schenken
Vern Schuppan

FORMULA ONE IS A MIGHTY SMALL POND CROWDED WITH a lot of hungry fish.

In the early 1970s, two Australians and a New Zealander were circling. Howden Ganley, Tim Schenken and Vern Schuppan achieved 78 world championship starts for nine Formula One teams over seven years. At different times, Schenken and Ganley had berths at Williams; Schenken and Schuppan drove for Surtees; Ganley and Schuppan raced with BRM. Between them they amassed seventeen world championship points and one podium.

Outside the Formula One pond they were hugely successful. Schuppan won the Le Mans 24 Hour and was third in the Indianapolis 500; Ganley was second at Le Mans; Schenken was part of Ferrari's World Sportscar Championship–winning team. All three won junior formulae. Ganley and Schenken started a company, Tiga ('Ti'—Tim, 'ga'—Ganley; pronounced 'tiger'), which designed and built 400 racing cars. Schuppan rented premises from them to build his Porsche-based road-going supercar. All three became major influencers in the sport: Ganley was

A double-breasted yachting jacket, an impeccable handmade tie and a breast-pocket handkerchief—hardly de rigueur for the F1 pits, yet Louis Stanley, chairman of BRM, wore them with imperious pride. Influential in the careers of Howden Ganley (pictured) and Vern Schuppan, he was, for all his pomposity, an early advocate of F1 safety and invested his company's funds in safety advances.

Not a lot of stability in the F1 of the '70s: Tim Schenken (left) and Howden Ganley, racing drivers turned race-car manufacturers. With Vern Schuppan, who joined their F1 'party' a little later, their careers were swept along on the fast-changing tides of sponsorship, and the patronage of wealthy enthusiasts and ambitious entrants.

secretary of the British Racing Drivers' Club, which runs Silverstone; Schenken became competitions director of Motorsport Australia; and Schuppan was a driving force behind bringing the Formula One world championship to Australia.

HOWDEN GANLEY

In Howden Ganley's first year as a Formula One driver, both his teammates perished in race crashes. Pedro Rodríguez's Ferrari 512M hit a bridge at the Norisring and caught fire. Jo Siffert's BRM overturned in a non-championship race at Brands Hatch. He suffered only a broken leg, but three fire extinguishers failed and he died of smoke inhalation before he could be freed. 'I was the third driver in the BRM team,' Ganley said from his COVID-19 isolation in a gated golfing community just east of San Francisco. 'When I went home to New

Howden Ganley's F1 career ended in 1974 when, driving for the Maki team, the fragile car crashed in its qualifying attempt at the Nürburgring. The Maki failed to qualify in another five world championship grands prix over two years and the team closed in 1976.

Zealand for Christmas that year, my mother said, "Two out of three isn't very good odds, is it?"'

Ganley was a survivor. His most horrific crash was also his last race in Formula One. The fragile Japanese-built Maki he was driving in the 1974 German Grand Prix at the Nürburgring broke its rear suspension on its first flying lap and turned at high speed into a barrier, tearing off the front end and leaving his legs exposed. Both were broken. 'There was the smell of fuel, so I got myself out and lay down in a ditch. It was maybe 15 minutes before medical help arrived. Every now and then a marshal would look down at me to see if I'd died.'

What sort of a name is Howden? 'Well, it's my mother's family name and as she had sisters the only way it was going to survive was if she gave it to me. I hated it as a kid, but it's kind of a racing driver's name, isn't it?' Howden grew up on the mighty Waikato River in Hamilton, New Zealand, racing the tiny P-class sailboats that taught all top Kiwi sailors to race. His first sight of a racing car in action was at the 1955 New Zealand Grand Prix on the Ardmore airstrip outside Auckland. The race was won by Prince Bira of Siam (Thailand), in a Maserati 250F, from Peter Whitehead and Tony Gaze in Ferraris. The blood-red Italian cars converted the thirteen-year-old. Sail gave way to power.

He club-raced his mother's Morris Minor, worked three jobs simultaneously, bought a Lotus 11 sports car (50:50 with his mother; together they paid $3000) and entered the 1961 New Zealand Grand Prix meeting, dominated by Jack Brabham and Bruce McLaren. Nineteen-year-old Ganley won the NZ Drivers Only race.

Two years later he wrapped the Lotus (worth $500,000 today) around a lamp pole in Dunedin and wiped out the capital he'd saved to fund a race program in the UK. He went anyway, relying on the generosity of others.

Bruce McLaren hired him, saying, 'I'm starting a race team and I want to stock it with Kiwis.' Howden became McLaren's fourth employee—not as a driver, but as a mechanic. 'Bruce was the most wonderful man,' Ganley said. 'We were working in rented premises on a dirt floor and all Bruce had was the Cooper with which he won the Tasman Series, and the Zerex Special sports car, but when we went testing at Goodwood he said, "Bring your helmet" and he gave me laps in the Cooper.'

Ganley was a talented technician. He helped develop race cars for McLaren, and Ford, on two continents. In 1969 he bought a Formula Three car and, like David Walker, went on the gypsy tour of the Continent. When he returned, McLaren introduced him to his neighbour Barry Newman, who was keen to sponsor him in McLaren's first F5000 car, the M10B. Ganley brought it home second in the British championship. Then Bruce McLaren died. 'I can't tell you where I was when JFK was shot,' Ganley said. 'But I know exactly where I was and how I felt when Bruce died. I was in our workshop. Barry Newman called me, screaming. He'd been at Goodwood.'

'We have several people with several protégés in this place,' Bruce McLaren had told Howden Ganley. 'You're mine.' Ganley says McLaren had promised him Formula One drives in 1970. Now the protégés of other directors came to the fore and Ganley was out.

Ganley knows how to talk the talk. It's one of his strengths. He courted Louis Stanley, the Colonel Blimp–like brother-in-law of Sir Alfred Owen, owner of BRM; and, although a non-smoker, Ganley made a point of becoming a trusted inner-circle confidante of the two tobacco companies that simultaneously sponsored the BRM team. In 1971, he claimed fifteenth in the world championship for

Howden Ganley's best world championship series was 1972. His connection with the tobacco giants that ruled F1 at the time provided him with a strong negotiating position with the teams he chose, but they let him down.

Yardley (owned by British American Tobacco), then in 1972 he was thirteenth for Marlboro (owned by rival Philip Morris).

'So many cartons of cigarettes would arrive home. I'd give them to Chris Amon.' Amon was a chain-smoker.

Louis Stanley—they called him 'Big Lou'—was chairman of BRM on behalf of his brother-in-law. He was a man of immense exaggeration and, according to those who drove for him, of extraordinary perfidy. 'BRM was overstretched, and Big Lou's promises for 1973 hadn't rung true,' Howden said. 'Marlboro asked me where I'd like to go—"We'll pay," they said.'

Having a moneyed sponsor in your pocket is something special. 'I settled on Frank Williams and the Iso-Ford project.' Williams cycled nine drivers through his team that year and Ganley was the only one who went full season, but it was full of jeopardy. 'I realised these guys were trying to kill me,' he said. 'Things were falling off. They had a crazy mechanic who'd never do things up with a spanner.' Ganley had a monstrous crash at the Nürburgring in qualifying. 'It went straight on at 180 mph [288 km/h]. The rear brake caliper had fallen off.'

Ganley had been working on his own car design and had it half-built: 'I offered to give it to them, free of charge, but Frank wouldn't have it.' Ganley salvaged a single championship point out of the season and finished nineteenth. Then he split with Williams 'by mutual agreement'.

In 1974, he received a phone call from Japan ('I thought it was Tim Schenken winding me up'). The promise from the just-formed Maki team was huge, but the outcome was not. Another crash at the Nürburgring—the one that broke both his legs—ended his career. 'Big Lou visited me in hospital,' Ganley said, still a little puzzled as to why.

'Mike Hailwood, who'd had his own crash, was in the next bed. Big Lou asked us what he could do. We said, "Get us home." By next morning he'd persuaded BOAC to put two stretchers on a flight, arranged all the paperwork, booked us into St Thomas' Hospital in London and had a top surgeon [the one who looked after Stirling Moss] waiting for us. There was nothing in it for him . . . maybe a bit of prestige. You just never know.'

TIM SCHENKEN

In 1971, Tim Schenken, 27, 'replaced' Jack Brabham as the next Australian in the Brabham F1 team. He joined two-time world champion Graham Hill. 'Graham didn't share much, but I learned a lot by just watching him,' Schenken mused. Schenken scored the team's only podium, third in the Austrian Grand Prix, and that makes him, still, only the fifth Australian podium place-getter in history alongside Brabham, Alan Jones, Mark Webber and Daniel Ricciardo. Except, Schenken recalled, 'there was no podium—just a party afterwards'. They were different times. Schenken was fourteenth in the world title that year. Hill, who suffered a run of retirements, was 21st.

Schenken grew up idolising not Jack Brabham but Stirling Moss. He went with his father to the 1956 Australian Grand Prix at Albert Park, which was won by Moss, and came home with Moss's autograph and a swatch of red paint from his Maserati. It's a souvenir he still cherishes. He 'stole' his mother's car (a Simca Aronde) for early illicit events, won the 1965 Australian Hill Climb Championship

Tim Schenken was a Brabham driver, the next after Jack—that's a big deal. In the 1971 British Grand Prix, driving the team's year-old BT33 design, he led good friend Ronnie Peterson (March Ford) before the Brabham broke its gearbox. Peterson finished second.

in a 500cc motorcycle-engine special, then raced a Lotus 18. Lex Davison invited him to join his Ecurie Australie, but Davison and his protégé Rocky Tresise were killed in successive weekends, leaving no team to join. David McKay, so prominent in the careers of young Australian and New Zealand drivers, said, 'Go overseas,' and equipped him with letters of introduction.

In England: 'We lived in a bedsit, four of us with mattresses on the floor.' Schenken raced an old Lotus 22 bought from a driving school and kept it going with 'parts from the school's rubbish bin'. His big break came when he was discovered by former racer Rodney Bloor of Manchester. 'His wife Denise and their three daughters treated me as a family member,' Schenken said. With the backing of Bloor's Sports Motors, the precocious talent ('I probably had an ego') won both the British Lombank Formula Ford series and the British Formula Three series in 1968, then backed up to win F3 again in 1969. 'There were 68 races in 1968 and I won 40 of them.'

Tim Schenken (left) and two-time world champion Graham Hill (right) interacted on multiple levels. In 1971 they were simultaneously teammates in Ron Tauranac's Brabham F1 team and in Ron Dennis's Rondel F2 team which used a Brabham BT36 chassis. The next year Hill stayed with Brabham and Schenken remained with Dennis (as well as joining John Surtees), ultimately driving Dennis's first purpose-built Rondel F2 car. Almost certainly Schenken and Hill did not share similar taste in hats.

In 1970, Piers Courage, heir to the Courage Brewery, died in a heavy, ill-handling, De Tomaso–built Williams F1 car in the Dutch Grand Prix, in a magnesium fire so intense that nearby trees were set alight. Schenken was faced with the ambitious racing driver's dilemma—whether or not to seek opportunity from tragedy. 'I worked up the nerve to go and see Frank Williams. Maybe others were too nervous to do it,' Schenken admits, and it resulted in four uncomfortable drives in Williams' De Tomaso in the last rounds of the world championship. 'There was no room for my elbows in the cockpit and there was horrendous kickback from the steering wheel.' In Schenken's second race, the

Italian Grand Prix, Jochen Rindt was killed. 'I'd come to know him well. It was terribly confusing. This was the sport I was so passionate about. You can only tell yourself—it's not going to happen to me.' He completed the season without being classified as a finisher.

The move to Brabham the next year felt 'so much more normal'. He was an Australian in what was essentially an Australian team and it was his best season in Formula One. At the end of the year Ron Tauranac sold Brabham to Bernie Ecclestone. 'I went to see Bernie and sought a one-year contract,' Schenken said, 'but he wanted two—"I'm not going to have you for one, just for you to bugger off," he said.' Schenken moved to Surtees: 'It proved not to be a good decision.'

John Surtees is unique—the only competitor ever to win the world championship on two wheels and four. 'He was a strange character. His attitude was almost one of paranoia,' Schenken said, a view supported by all who drove for him.

Ron Tauranac hired Tim Schenken in 1971, as number two to former world champion Graham Hill, yet Schenken scored the Brabham team's only podium that year, and the team claimed ninth in the World Constructors' Championship. Faced with mounting costs, Tauranac sold the team to Bernie Ecclestone.

Surtees rotated four drivers that season—one was Mike Hailwood, his fellow motorcycle world champion. 'At the British Grand Prix, I outqualified Mike,' Schenken recalled. 'I expected John to say something nice, but what he said was: "On our timing, Mike was faster than you. I'm going to protest [the official time] and sort it out."' The time stood; Schenken started fifth, Hailwood seventh, but they both retired with mechanical failure.

In 1974, British industrialist Peter Agg contracted Ron Tauranac to build a Formula One kit car for private buyers. The car was called Trojan and Schenken was hired as its sole works driver. In six starts, it claimed two tenths and a fourteenth. Tauranac was blunt in his assessment of Schenken's ability: 'Our driver had recently married, and I think that modified his views of the risk business,' he said. Schenken had met Brigitte at Hockenheim in 1972 (she was there with one of Mike Hailwood's many girlfriends). Tauranac later recanted, at least slightly: 'The rear-suspension geometry was not ideal either.'

Schenken led a parallel life to Formula One. He joined a roster of exceptional talent to drive for Ferrari in the World Sportscar Championship, then called the World Championship for Makes. He gravitated to partnership with Ronnie Peterson. They won the world championship for the 'make', but there was no driver recognition.

'Ronnie was an amazing driver,' Tim said. 'Brigitte and I and our son Guido were with Ronnie, [his wife] Barbro and their daughter Nina in Monaco for Guido's birthday the week before the 1978 Italian Grand Prix. We knew them so well.' Ronnie died as a result of injuries in that race. Tim had retired in 1977.

VERN SCHUPPAN

Vern Schuppan has a different take on the interference of past champions in the running of their race teams—why title holders John Surtees and Graham Hill were such uncompromising martinets: 'There was no data acquisition in those days,' Schuppan said. 'Without defined reference points, they figured *they* set the standard. The problem was that as soon as you're out of a race car for a while, you lose your pace. Generally, they were a lot slower than we were, and a car's set-up relies on those last few seconds of pace.'

Schuppan was a late starter compared to Schenken and Ganley. He arrived in Europe two years after them and remained in Formula One a little longer. 'I set a target that I would win a major championship within two years of leaving home and I would be in Formula One within four years.' He achieved both.

Schuppan was from Whyalla on South Australia's Spencer Gulf. The first motor race he saw was the 1955 Australian Grand Prix held just around the gulf

Vern Schuppan was one of Australia's most versatile drivers—winner of the 1983 Le Mans 24 Hour race, third in the 1981 Indianapolis 500, winner of the 1976 Tasman Series, F5000 winner at Brands Hatch (pictured)—but, frustratingly, he never made the podium in Formula One.

at Port Wakefield, won by Jack Brabham. An early adopter of go-karts, Schuppan won three South Australian championships. Then, with wife Jennifer, he loaded a kitted-out Ford 10 van onto the *Angelina Lauro* and headed for the UK. It was 1969, Vern was 26 (old to be starting a motor-racing career), and they'd saved about $4000 to fund their adventure.

Tim Schenken and Howden Ganley welcomed the new boy warmly, then pointed him in the wrong direction. 'Tim told me to go production sports racing,' Vern recalled. 'It was a ticket to nowhere.'

Instead, Vern spent just under $2000 on a very used Alexis Formula Ford; at his first meeting at Oulton Park, he was twelfth in a gun field of 32. BRM, which built engines for all categories, offered him an engine deal, but he declined a second year in Formula Ford, moved up a category ('I had a plan') and won the inaugural British Formula Atlantic Championship in 1971. It was a direct stepping stone to Formula One.

'Big Lou Stanley said he'd give me a Formula One test if I won the Atlantic series,' Vern said. It turned out the 'test' was a race—the non-championship Gold Cup at Oulton Park. 'The first time I drove a Formula One car was in a race.' Incredible. Even more so, he came fifth. Denny Hulme won, and Tim Schenken

Mo Nunn's Ensign team—funded by Vern Schuppan's patron Teddy Yip, a Macau casino owner—could have been Schuppan's F1 salvation. Instead it netted just a fifteenth place in the 1974 Belgian Grand Prix and Schuppan, concerned for his safety, moved on to Graham Hill's team the following season.

was third. Vern had achieved his F1 goal ten months shy of his 30th birthday goal. The next weekend, Big Lou took him to the Belgian Grand Prix, fully intending to run him in a fourth car, with teammates Howden Ganley, Peter Gethin and Helmut Marko. It would be his first world championship.

But teammate Peter Gethin crashed in practice, so, like a row of falling dominos, Helmut Marko gave his car to Gethin and took over Schuppan's. Ganley clung to his BRM throughout. The new boy got to watch as Ganley claimed eighth and Marko came tenth. Schuppan's consolation was a start in the non-championship World Championship Victory Race at Brands Hatch, and he was fourth, directly ahead of Gethin.

Big Lou summoned Schuppan to his suite at The Dorchester in London. (Big Lou did a convincing impersonation of royalty. In the US, he liked to be known as Lord Stanley.) Over high tea he presented Vern with a contract for the 1973 F1 season. His teammates would be Jean-Pierre Beltoise and Clay Regazzoni.

'Jennifer and I went back to Australia for Christmas and when we returned, I opened the *Daily Express* at Heathrow Airport to discover Niki Lauda was in the team as well.' The young Lauda had bought a drive from Stanley on a lay-by plan. 'We went to the media announcement at Marlboro's headquarters in Geneva, and a journalist noted that there were four drivers and three cars,' Vern said. 'We shall field a fourth car,' Big Lou retorted imperiously.

It didn't happen. The closest Schuppan came was the paradoxically named Race of Champions, a non-championship race, at Brands Hatch where he shared the front row with Lauda and Beltoise but retired after being forced off the track. In his first three F1 races, Schuppan had qualified fifth, then fourth, then third—on the right trajectory.

But he spent the 1973 championship year as a test and reserve driver for BRM—'They used to pay £500 [A$850] a day for testing'—and raced in other series around the world as well. The money was good. It bought him a Ferrari. 'I was down in Monaco for the grand prix and popped across to Maranello to pick up my new Dino [£4600/A$7900], and I was taken to meet Mr Ferrari, who said, "I hope one day you will drive for me."' That didn't happen either, but it's an indication of Schuppan's wide-eyed sincerity and respect for the sport then and now that he rates the encounter as a highlight in his career.

In 1974, Schuppan endured half a season in Mo Nunn's underdog Ensign team. It was a struggle to qualify. He raced twice at the Nürburgring in three months, in two starkly different experiences. In May, with Gulf Racing's sports-car team, he was paired with James Hunt and was fourth in the 1000-kilometre World Championship for Makes race. In August, in the German Grand Prix, his Ensign's throttle jammed wide open. 'I informed Mo that I didn't need Formula One that badly and would no longer drive for him.'

Graham Hill called him up for one race in 1975 to sub for the injured Rolf Stommelen. The race was in Sweden and Hill flew his team across in his own plane: 'Does anyone know what Anderstorp looks like from the air?' he enquired, perhaps only partly joking. The plane had feathered one propellor on the way across when Hill neglected to switch fuel tanks. Schuppan had no more joy with the Embassy Hill. It stopped mid-race.

'I was in America in 1977 racing for Dan Gurney when I took a phone call from John Surtees,' Vern said. 'Larry Perkins had not been able to qualify the Surtees TS19 in two races and he asked me to take his place.' Why? 'Well, why

Judy Kondratieff Ganley was an accomplished sports-car racer (voted Woman Racer of the Year by the Californian Motorsports Press Association), and an amazing lap chart-keeper and team manager—renowned for being able to accurately time twenty cars simultaneously with one stopwatch. She managed teams for Chris Amon, Vern Schuppan and her husband.

---

wouldn't you?' Schuppan retorted. 'I was a professional racing driver and I rarely refused a drive.'

He brought the car home seventh in the German Grand Prix but ran into the brick wall of Surtees' intractable attitude. One example: 'We'd been testing without John and tried a new nose cone that wasn't on his to-do list. It made us 2 seconds a lap faster, but when we got back to the factory, he was livid that we did it without his permission. He punished his test manager by not letting him go to the next GP.'

Schuppan left the team with four races remaining. 'I wanted to be in Formula One with a car and a team that was going somewhere. Ultimately, it's a matter of all the stars aligning. Alan Jones got it right. When he moved from Shadow to Williams it looked like a backward move. I'd done some testing for Frank Williams and at the time I wouldn't have put him up there as someone who was going to further your career. But it all came together—right designer, right car, right team. They had the Saudi money and Alan became world champion.' No regrets. Schuppan had already forged a solid career and he went on to make it stellar. 'There were a lot of things to do in motor racing beyond Formula One.'

Ganley, Schenken and Schuppan enjoy positions of eminence within motorsport. All three are members of the Club International des Anciens Pilotes de Grand Prix F1, an exclusive association started during the time of Juan Manuel Fangio. Tiga, the company Ganley and Schenken built, was sold on after the partners tired of the grind of customer care. The cars they built are in high demand for historic racing. Ganley became one of the driving forces in turning around the fortunes of the British Racing Drivers' Club and its circuit, Silverstone, but retired when his wife Judy fell ill. Ganley and Judy Kondratieff, a prominent American racer, were married for 37 years; she died from ovarian cancer in 2007. Schenken accepted a role with CAMS, now Motorsport Australia, and is race director of Supercars and Clerk of the Course at the annual Australian Grand Prix. Until his enforced retirement at age 75, he was an influential member of many committees within the FIA.

10

LP AND PEEWEE
Larry Perkins
Greg Siddle

LARRY PERKINS' FORMULA ONE CAREER SPANNED THREE years, five teams and fifteen races but in the turbulent mid-1970s, as underfunded and badly managed teams jostled for grid positions, The Cowangie Kid chose poorly, got carved up by international interests and was let down by unkept promises. Perkins, though, has a special place as a trailblazer. He was instrumental in the formation of RALT, Ron Tauranac's racing-car business, and laid the DNA trail for a succession of Formula One drivers—including two world champions who used Tauranac's cars as their nursery.

When Larry 'LP' Perkins met Greg 'Peewee' Siddle in London in 1974 ('Peewee' because of his size but also, he claims, he resembled Ian 'Peewee' Wilson, lead singer of the 1960s surf band The Delltones), Peewee had already determined he was not going to be a world champion. But he was an Aussie can-do sort of bloke, capable of lifting and carrying for Perkins. His home in Acton, west London, became a revolving door for Formula One aspirants from Down Under.

Larry Perkins drove the Gordon Murray—designed Brabham BT45 in the 1976 Canadian and US Grands Prix as well as in the infamously wet Japanese Grand Prix, Perkins was approaching the lap averages of his Brabham teammate Carlos Pace, but his contract was not renewed for 1977.

Peewee Siddle, who was 'never a manager', was a major influence in the career of three-time world champion Nelson Piquet (left). Between them, in shadow, is multiple Australian Grand Prix winner Roberto Moreno, another Brazilian to receive 'the Peewee push'. Moreno's Australian Grand Prix wins came before they were part of the world title.

Peewee went on to become an influencer within the sport. 'I was never in Formula One,' he claimed, straight-faced, so disingenuously it was gob smacking. This is the man who guided Nelson Piquet through three world titles ('never managed him, only helped') and whose number was in Bernie Ecclestone's teledex. Ron Tauranac was the glue that bound Perkins and Siddle. When Tauranac died in 2020, both paid special tribute at his memorial.

Perkins grew up in the Mallee of north-west Victoria, outside the dusty town of Cowangie—hence his nickname. His dad was Eddie Perkins, winner of the 1956 Round Australia Trial, a bloke who raced in shorts and workman's boots. Even today, Perkins plays on the image—the humble windmill mechanic in stubbies and Blunnies, greeting his guests in the marble foyer of his St Kilda Road apartment.

As a kid, Perkins turned dominance in Formula Vee into an Australian Formula Ford Series victory for four-time Australian Drivers' Champion (and millionaire) Bib Stillwell; then won the Australian Formula

Larry Perkins, The Cowangie Kid—never quite the naive Mallee-country boy of his image—was a gifted driver and engineer, recognised in the 2021 Queen's Birthday Honours List as a member of the Order of Australia (AM).

Two Championship for racer and motor dealer Gary Campbell. He courted David McKay, a friend of his father, whose Scuderia Veloce had fielded Eddie in the 1968 London–Sydney Marathon. McKay used his influence, and some of his and Campbell's money, to fund a modest European Formula Three assault. McKay persuaded David Walker, a former star pupil, to help Perkins into a well-used GRD. Perkins hauled the GRD to races 'in an old black Bedford furniture van,' Siddle recalled, 'and a bloke offered him a job to cart furniture during the week'.

In 1974 McKay recommended Perkins to another former pupil, Chris Amon, who was about to start his own Formula One team. Perkins joined Amon as a mechanic and as a proposed teammate. It was his first Formula One false start.

First up, they went to the fearsome Nürburgring. Amon drove the Amon AF101 in practice, then fell ill. Perkins took over. 'I came over the hill at Adenau

Larry Perkins berated himself for this slight altercation with the catch fences, which proliferated in Formula One in the mid-1970s. Drafted into the Brabham BT45 for the US and Canadian rounds of the 1976 series, he was praised by the media for his neat and tidy job. He outqualified Alan Jones (Surtees) in both North American races.

and it was raining on the other side,' he told the *V8 Sleuth* podcast. 'It speared off and I banged it. We had no spares, and the car was withdrawn.' The Amon team shut down soon after.

Ron Tauranac was on gardening leave when Larry Perkins got in touch. Tauranac had sold Motor Racing Developments at the end of 1971 to Bernie Ecclestone.

'I'd met Ron in 1971 in Melbourne and he said if I got to England to give him a call,' Perkins recalled in his eulogy at Tauranac's memorial service. 'He asked me around to his home and he and Norma gave me lunch.'

It was a bit overwhelming—'I was a nobody, and he was Mr Big'—but Tauranac offered to help with Perkins' GRD. There was nothing in it for him; he was just

A lifetime of friendship, cemented by their mutual mentor Ron Tauranac. Larry Perkins (left) and Greg 'Peewee' Siddle at the 2017 Australian Grand Prix. By then Perkins had won the Bathurst 1000 six times, three with Peter Brock and the Holden Dealer Team and three with his own team.

magnanimous. This was, according to Peewee Siddle, typical Tauranac. For all his tough-as-nails reputation, he was exceptionally supportive of people with the right stuff.

'One day he called me and said he was starting up RALT,' Perkins said. 'Just working out of his garage, nothing flash. I said I could bring a truck and engines to the deal, and he could provide the car.' Perkins put the RT1 on pole at Thruxton in its first event in 1975, then spun out while leading ('Ron wasn't pleased'). But Perkins won the six-round European Formula Three Cup in RALT's inaugural year and came fifth in the British Formula Three title. He lost the Monaco F3 race—the most important race of the year—only because David McKay got excited. Perkins was in the box seat and 'David was all for signalling him with the news,' Tauranac said in his biography. 'I told him not to because I know drivers and I figured that Larry would lose concentration. David ignored my advice, hung out the pit board and sure enough, Larry crashed.'

Just the same, RALT was an overnight success, against the might of the entrenched March organisation (a race team owned in part by later FIA president Max Mosley), and Perkins was back on the Formula One map.

'If I had a mentor it was Ron,' Peewee Siddle recalled. 'He was tough to work with, but I never worked for him.' (Of course not.) Nonetheless, Siddle guided a lot of aspirants through the gates. Some, like Nelson Piquet, were well equipped with funds. Others were poor. Geoff Brabham looked like he was doing it tough until 1975 Australian Formula Ford champion Paul Bernasconi showed up: 'Geoff had a Goodyear deal,' Bernasconi said. 'After he'd used up his tyres he'd give them to me and I'd use them some more. Then I'd give the carcasses back, so Geoff could trade them for new ones.' Bernasconi used to rent his RALT to others to race for £3000 [A$4700] a time so he could, occasionally, afford to race it himself. They all worked out of RALT's workshop, courtesy of Ron Tauranac's kindness. And they all succeeded, in one form or other, because of what became known as the 'Peewee push'.

In later days you'd look back on it: whether it was Bob Jane wanting to bring Niki Lauda to Australia to race at Calder, Alan Webber wanting to test his son Mark in Formula Ford ('Don't bring your boy back here for more testing—buy him a race car,' Siddle advised), or a passing parade of cashed-up Brazilians with high hopes, the fine touch of Peewee was, perhaps, on the deal; always straight up, never shady, but undeniably deniable.

On the strength of his RALT success, Perkins dived back into the Formula One pond. He miscued with Boro, a team owned by two Dutch brothers. He scored an eighth in the Belgian Grand Prix before they went broke. Then Carlos Reutemann left Brabham to go to Ferrari and Bernie Ecclestone called Perkins. 'I was young enough to be a bit faster than I should have been,' Perkins recalled. Driving at '110 per cent', he skidded the Brabham mildly into a catch fence in the US Grand Prix ('it doesn't look good on your CV'), then retired with suspension failure, and out-practised his teammate Carlos Pace in the first session

Larry Perkins (Boro) plunges down the hill at Zandvoort in the 1976 Dutch Grand Prix, hotly pursued by two-time world champion Emerson Fittipaldi in the Copersucar designed by Australian Ralph Bellamy. Neither finished. Perkins drove the Boro, a rebadged and ultimately rebuilt Ensign, in six races in 1976 before moving to the Brabham team.

of the infamous wet 1976 Japanese Grand Prix. Like Niki Lauda, he started but withdrew from the event. In 1977, Martini, the team's main sponsors, decided they wanted a European driver to enhance their image. The Cowangie Kid, simply, was 'not Martini friendly'.

At the start of 1977, Larry raced with Big Lou Stanley, a well-worn path for the Down Under contingent, but the car had 'a shocking design failure. The radiators were so small you wouldn't put them on a Mini Minor. I wasn't out of sight of the pits in Brazil when the car was boiling'. He finished the season with Surtees—another 'great disappointment'.

David McKay called it in his autobiography: '[Perkins'] shot at F1 was effectively at an end.' McKay remained a big fan; in his curiously old-world way, he wrote: 'Larry's driving and his qualities as a man weren't dimmed.' It had been character building for Perkins. 'I'd planned my whole life on doing Formula One and now it wasn't going to happen,' he said. But he'd learned a lot.

In Formula One, he'd been exposed to the worst of team management and the worst of car preparation. 'It was quite a learning experience to find such shocking examples of engineering and the standards of the mechanics. That's why when I came back to Australia, I determined I'd run [my team] and there'd be only one person to blame then if it didn't work.' He won the Bathurst 1000 six times: three times with Peter Brock, and when he left Brock's organisation, three times again in his own right. One of those wins was, exceptionally, from last place.

Perkins did return to Europe. Sports-car racing at its very elite level has been a parallel path for Down Under racers. Tony Gaze started it all, racing Aston Martins for the Kangaroo Stable in 1955; Jack Brabham raced at Le Mans three times between 1957 and 1970; Frank Gardner and Paul Hawkins made much of their living racing sports cars; Tim Schenken helped Ferrari win the 1972 World Sportscar Championship; and Bruce McLaren and Chris Amon famously won the big one, Le Mans, in 1966, with Denny Hulme and Ken Miles in second. Vern Schuppan won Le Mans for Porsche in 1983. A decade later Geoff Brabham would win for Peugeot, and sixteen years after that his brother David would win it for the same marque. Later again, Brendon Hartley would win it twice, once for Porsche and once for Toyota. Mark Webber became world endurance champion in 2015, teamed with Hartley.

Perkins raced at Le Mans first in 1978. It was a class car, not an outright contender, and as one of three drivers in the Charles Ivey team he brought the Porsche 911 Carrera RS home second in category and fourteenth outright.

In 1984, Alan Jones accepted an offer from the Porsche Kremer team to race in the outright category. It seemed only logical that Perkins should have a crack

Larry Perkins raced twice in the Le Mans 24 Hours. In 1984 he paired with Peter Brock in Team Australia, entered by John Fitzpatrick and funded by Bob Jane, but their Porsche 956 failed during the night. Fitzpatrick's sister car came third. Four years later Perkins went back with Tom Walkinshaw's Jaguar team and came home a meritorious fourth.

too. The catalyst was Peter Brock. Brock had been to Le Mans eight years earlier, racing a BMW CSL. It had failed to finish but fuelled Brock's desire to have one of his 'red hot goes'. For Le Mans in '84, Brock found funding from tyre magnate Bob Jane, leased a Porsche 956 from former Bathurst 1000 winner John Fitzpatrick, secured Perkins as teammate and launched an essentially privateer attempt to win a race that was the domain of the works teams. The car failed, then crashed in the middle of the night; Jones, in a works car, finished sixth. Lesson learned.

In 1988 Larry Perkins went back to Le Mans, this time as part of Tom Walkinshaw's works Jaguar team. Along with Derek Daly and Kevin Cogan, both Formula One drivers, he brought the Silk Cut Jaguar XJR-9 home fourth.

Perkins' years in Europe, working largely with underperforming, try-hard teams, had been a salutary lesson in how not to do it. But with the backing of a true works operation, Perkins proved he had the goods. If only he'd gotten the breaks all those years before.

11

DRIVING AMBITION— OUR LATEST WORLD CHAMPION
Alan Jones
Brian McGuire

THEY WERE BEST MATES, CHILDHOOD FRIENDS, AND they'd sailed to the UK on the grand motor-racing adventure together. One would become world champion. The other would die at the wheel of a Formula One car.

Alan Jones and Brian McGuire had grown up together. McGuire's dad Bill was spare-parts manager for the Holden dealership owned by Jones' dad, Stan. The mezzanine above the workshop was the kids' weekend domain. They'd buy Chiko Rolls and chips, and eat them up there, where they'd plot mischief. Their dads liked that. Stan Jones, who had won the Australian and New Zealand grands prix, and the 1958 Australian Drivers' Championship, was no shrinking violet.

Stan was one of the toughest and most talented drivers his country had produced, 'faster and better than Brabham', his son Alan proudly proclaimed.

Alan Jones was forceful and aggressive. His strategy, always, was to win from the front. In the 1980 Belgian Grand Prix at Zolder, he leaped to take the lead from Jacques Laffite (Ligier JS11). It was driving like this that won Alan the 1980 world title, even though he finished second at Zolder.

Alan Jones learned his racecraft from his father, Stan. That's Alan standing proudly alongside his dad. Stan won the 1954 New Zealand Grand Prix, the 1959 Australian Grand Prix and the 1958 Australian Gold Star Championship. He competed in the 1953 Monte Carlo Rally but never raced in European Formula One.

He was also a tearaway. He'd rather have a fight than a feed, and was in and out of money—but when he had it, he was the most generous man alive. Alan, part of Stan's crew as a kid, and photographed with him at his dad's victories, misses him to this day.

Stan gifted his son a stove-hot Mini Cooper racing car and then, when the lad did okay, let him dust off his 2.2-litre Cooper Climax open-wheeler and race that as well. It was, perhaps, his way of compensating. The Jones household was fractured by domestic violence and then divorce. Stan was a big-time drinker and philanderer. He gave his son lessons in life not by word but by deed: he made him obstinate, and very definitely a sore loser, both perfect qualities for a Formula One driver.

'Get yourself out of here, go to the UK,' Stan told his boy. Stan used to say that he always wished he'd gone; 50 years on, Alan—in his completely pragmatic way—says: 'If he'd really wanted to, he would have.' Stan promised to send Alan money, but it never arrived. He'd gone bust in Australia. Several years later, Stan turned up in the UK, desperately ill, already the victim of two strokes, a shadow of his former self but still full of fire. He died, aged 49, in the care of Alan's then-wife Beverley while Alan was at a Formula Three race meeting at Silverstone.

Jones and McGuire were go-getters. They'd learned to hard-sell on the car lots of Melbourne. In England they began recycling mini-vans and campers through a swirling pool of young Australian and New Zealand backpackers. They'd buy the vans, do them up, and sell them with a guaranteed buyback on their return; then, a bit naughtily, they'd pay far less and pocket the difference.

That made them enough to buy a locally built Merlyn Formula Ford, which they shared. McGuire wrote it off. Jones bought a Lotus 41, and he wrote that off too, and broke his leg. It was time to stop mucking about. In 1971 the pair bought two last-season Brabham BT28 Formula Three cars and had Ron Tauranac update them to current specifications. Then they bought an old furniture van, painted it orange and lettered it with the decals of the Australian International Racing Organisation (AIRO)—their own invention—and went racing for starting money.

Jones was the better driver, and certainly the more committed. McGuire's attention was tangential. He was always keeping one eye on the campervan business that was funding them. You can't do that and be successful at either. Jones, frankly, didn't give a damn. He was living for today's result and tomorrow's opportunity. Later, when Alan entered Formula One, Brian had to have an F1 car too. There was an element of keeping up with Jones.

McGuire bought two redundant race cars from Frank Williams—the 1975 FW04, strictly a privateer effort. The cars had been unloved by Willams' drivers. But McGuire was buoyed by winning the Thruxton round of the 1976 Shellsport International Series—the British domestic Formula One series. He set his sights on the big time. He entered the 1977 world championship British Grand Prix at Silverstone. If he qualified, he'd be racing at the pinnacle of

Victory and tragedy in a fortnight. In 1977, Brian McGuire (left) joined a small but significant roll call of drivers who died in their attempt to enter Formula One competition. On 14 August his friend Alan Jones had won his first world championship Formula One race, the Austrian Grand Prix. Fifteen days later McGuire (pictured in practice for the 1977 British Grand Prix) had a fatal crash at Brands Hatch when his brake pedal snapped.

the sport, against Jones. He slightly modified the old cars and renamed them the McGuire BM1.

'I warned him, "This isn't like a junior-category car,"' Jones said, all these years later. 'A Formula One car has pressures on it the smaller classes don't experience. It's why the works teams strip them down and rebuild them after every race. You have to be bloody careful.'

In July, McGuire failed to qualify for the British Grand Prix. His time of 1 min 23.76 seconds was 4.3 seconds slower than Jones, who claimed twelfth grid position. McGuire didn't make the cut. Disappointed but undeterred, he entered the domestic F1 series. The following month he was testing at Brands

Hatch when a fulcrum pin broke on the brake pedal and, unretarded, he crashed. He and a track marshal were killed.

'Brian's death affected me, but it didn't stop me,' Jones recalled in our conversation for this book. He compartmentalised his friend's death: 'It wasn't Brian getting killed in a racing car. It was just Brian getting killed.'

Alan Jones did his best to stay out of the pond. There was no point in being part of the crowd. 'I always thought I was a level above. What was the point of doing it if I was only as good as them? Sounds arrogant,' he smiled. But there was more than a modicum of truth to it. Later in his career, Jones would go out of his way to stay in a different hotel, catch a different plane, not be seen with a drink in his hand in the days before a race. 'I'd never relax around the motor-racing crowd, never let my guard down.'

He made an exception for David Walker. Jones had first met Walker in Brazil when they were contesting a three-round local championship for a lot of money. It was Jones' first away-opportunity. Walker, five years older and a works Lotus F3 driver, pointed out—in a quiet, friendly, laconic fashion—that the inexperienced Jones had fitted his aerodynamic wing back to front. Jones corrected it, went quicker and joined Walker on the front row of the grid. Walker and Jones socialised a bit. Walker helped secure Jones a Formula Three drive with GRD, the Lotus breakaway team. Jones won in the GRD at Silverstone the day his father died. He placed his winner's garland into Stan's lead-lined coffin and sent him home for burial.

'It surprised me that David didn't do better with his Lotus Formula One opportunity,' Jones contemplated. 'He was seriously quick.' He was less complimentary about others.

In the last round of the 1973 European F3 championship, Jones needed fourth or better to win the title on points. He was holding that position, nursing a dying engine, when Larry Perkins went to pass. Jones went defensive and Perkins was punted off. 'But he came back on and this time he got me and cost me the championship, which went to Tony Brise,' Jones recalled. 'Fair enough. Then I heard Larry was going to protest me for dangerous driving. I fronted him in the clubhouse, and he said: "I hope I never have the displeasure of racing against you again." As it turned out we did share a Formula One grid, but we never raced. [Not quite true—they were competitive.] He never scored a point. We don't speak much even now but I like to remind him of that.'

Alan Jones' Formula One trajectory was lineal: a season with DART (Dobbie Automobile Racing Team) in Formula Three, second in the European title, a season in Harry Stiller's Formula Atlantic team, second in the British Formula Atlantic championship, and next season—the big time. Simple.

Harry Stiller was his conduit to Formula One. The former British F3 champion hired Jones to race his Formula Atlantic. Jones' win by the full length of the straight in the support race to the 1974 British Grand Prix clinched his commitment. Stiller was happy to invest in a Formula One opportunity.

Most Formula One teams ran their organisations out of converted factories. Hesketh, owned by Lord Alexander Hesketh and his lieutenant 'Bubbles' Horsley, was run from a castle. The team's number-one driver in 1975 was James Hunt, who would be world champion the following year. Hunt was mainstream A-list, a headline-attracting, beautifully spoken, globally recognised larrikin in torn jeans and a T-shirt. His wife Suzy would soon leave him for actor Richard

Grass cutting, the Jones way. Jack Brabham perfected the technique of using more than the available raceway to shave milliseconds off his time and deter following drivers. Alan Jones followed suit, as shown here in the 1975 Swedish Grand Prix—the first Formula One race he finished—driving the Hesketh 308B. He placed eleventh.

Burton. Jones would not be Hunt's teammate but rather work out of the same stable. 'Harry [Stiller] had a lot of money in our car,' Jones said. Six races into the season, Jones was matching Hunt's pace ('nobody offered a lot of advice') and Hesketh told Jones that he'd run two cars the following year—one for Hunt and one for Jones. Then Stiller ran out of money. More accurately, he ran out of Britain, closely pursued by the tax authorities. But opportunity arose.

There'd been a huge crash in the Spanish Grand Prix in Montjuïc Park in Barcelona. Rolf Stommelen's Embassy Hill had a rear-wing strut failure and flew into the crowd, killing five spectators. Team owner Graham Hill secured Jones to substitute for the injured Stommelen—'The car wasn't as good as the Hesketh,' Jones said—and Jones was at odds with Hill. The two-time world champion would stubbornly not listen to his driver. It was difficult to effect change. Jones drove four times for Hill and claimed a fifth, and championship points, at the Nürburgring. They flew home in Hill's private aircraft and discussed testing later in the year in the south of France. On that flight, Jones became convinced Hill was a better race driver than he was a pilot.

The French test went ahead without Jones. Hill took Tony Brise, who'd beaten Jones in the Formula Atlantic Championship, instead. Landing back in England in fog, the aircraft flew into the side of a mound on a local golf course, killing all six on board. Hill was not licensed for night flying.

'Bastard. Why didn't he tell me?' Alan Jones joked. It was 1976 and Jones was about to take on a full season with 'Big' John Surtees. Tim Schenken had been there four years before. The least he could have done was warn a fellow Aussie. 'Surtees was a lunatic—he carried on like a complete chook. It's a pity, because his car was alright, maybe even a potential winner,' Jones said.

Jones got his first inkling of the year ahead when Surtees thrust a contract at him at Heathrow Airport prior to pre-season testing in South Africa. 'I'd like my lawyer to see it,' said Jones. 'Sign now or you're not going,' Surtees retorted. Jones signed. 'On the way down, I was sitting in the middle seat—John on one side, a lady on the other. She asked what I did, and I started to tell her.'

Jones recalled: 'Suddenly there was a dig in the ribs from John and a demand that I keep quiet: "She could be a plant." Like, seriously—Ferrari would put a spy on the plane to find out what I know?'

The Surtees team was controversial that year. It had found sponsorship from the London Rubber Company, which made condoms. To get to Jones at a grand prix, it was necessary to run the gauntlet of sportily dressed Durex promotions girls offering samples. It was a good promotion—safe sex balanced

against dangerous motor racing, all clean fun—but the puritanical BBC took such exception that it withdrew its cameras from Formula One.

Surtees' wrath spared no one. 'We'd had understeer all year courtesy of John's failure to understand how to progressively dial it out,' Jones said. 'One time he was called away and Mike Hailwood took the opportunity to put some aluminium skirting around the nose. It fixed the problem and found half a second a lap. When John got back, he blew up and demanded it be taken off—simply because he had not authorised it.' Jones' problem was even more visceral. 'I wanted a bubble in the bodywork so I could change gears without scraping my knuckles. It wasn't just that it hurt—I was missing gears. I fought and fought until John said—"Okay, I understand, we'll incorporate it in the car next year." He didn't want to spoil the symmetry of this year's car by having a bubble only on one side.'

Jones' best result for Surtees was saved for the final race of the year—fourth in the rain-soaked 1976 Japanese Grand Prix, in which James Hunt won the world championship after Niki Lauda pulled out. ('If I'd been Niki, I would have just trundled around, never given up.') Jones raced into fifteenth place in the world title and advanced Surtees to tenth in the World Constructors' Championship,

Opposite: Monaco Grand Prix, 1976: Alan Jones spent a full, frustrating season in world champion John Surtees' Durex team. The obstinate Surtees, in the car, seldom listened to his drivers, preferring to drive the car himself in private practice and set it up to his own liking.

Above: In 1977, at the Austrian Grand Prix, Alan Jones was nine races into his season with Don Nichols' Shadow team when he won his, and Shadow's, first grand prix. Jones was in the ascendancy; Shadow was heading the other way, and was absorbed into Teddy Yip's Theodore Racing. Shadow's principal sponsor, Italian businessman Franco Ambrosio, was much later jailed for financial crimes and murdered in a robbery at his home.

then spent the Australian summer dodging Big John, who wanted to exercise his contractual right to take him up for a second year.

He was sitting out the 1977 season when Welshman Tom Pryce was killed at Kyalami in his Shadow DN8, his head impacted at 270 km/h with a fire extinguisher carried by a nineteen-year-old marshal who died too. Shadow team owner Don Nichols picked holes in Surtees' contract and Jones took Pryce's place.

Nine races later he won his first grand prix. 'Don Nichols had a sweet tooth—every meeting involved two boxes of chocolate biscuits. It's strange how you remember these things,' Jones recalled. The car was a bit soft too. The cash-strapped team progressively stripped it of weight and on the fast, hilly Österreichring (now called the Red Bull Ring), Jones worked his way up from fourteenth grid position to beat hometown hero Niki Lauda by 20 seconds. 'It was raining, and I like the rain' is his recollection and only explanation. The Australian victory took organisers by surprise. They didn't have a recording of the Australian national anthem, so they played 'Happy Birthday' instead.

Don Nichols wanted Alan Jones, seventh in the world title, to stay for 1978. But Jones was also in demand from Frank Williams and Enzo Ferrari. He was totally transparent. From Nichols, he wanted to be paid for 1977, never mind the following year. He told Frank Williams that Ferrari was interested and Williams agreed to wait. He flew to Maranello and signed an option with Ferrari, but they reneged, taking Gilles Villeneuve instead.

In 1980, Alan Jones became the first of Williams' world champions. Williams created seven champions, with no repeats, won nine constructors' titles and claimed 114 race victories (up to the beginning of the 2021 season). Williams Grand Prix Engineering was made for Alan Jones, and he was made for them.

'We couldn't afford one of the top names,' Frank Williams explained bluntly at the time. What he needed was a proven quantity with the right work ethic. Jones fitted the bill. Frank Williams had been a handy Formula Three competitor in the 1960s. In 1969, the natural salesman had found funding and fielded a team for his friend and flatmate Piers Courage. Halfway through their first Formula One season, Courage was killed in the team's De Tomaso. Williams carried on as a team owner.

In 1976, Canadian oil millionaire Walter Wolf bought 60 per cent of Williams Racing, merged it with assets he'd purchased from the disbanded Hesketh team and then, inexplicably, fired Frank. In February 1977, Frank regrouped and launched Williams Grand Prix Engineering. He owned 70 per cent of the company and he brought in young designer Patrick Head as minority shareholder. The FW06 that Jones drove in 1978 was the first car Head designed under the Williams masthead.

'I liked them both a lot. We were all about the same age'—Head was just four months older than Jones, and they looked like twins—'and they had a plan,' Jones said. Williams promised he would build the team around Jones. For the first year at least, he would be the sole driver. It helped that Saudi Arabian interests had offered support—Williams had tapped an enthusiastic and lucrative market, keen

The moment it became official. Alan Jones confirmed his 1980 world championship at the US Grand Prix at Watkins Glen. His win in Canada the week before had made his title unassailable, and Williams had wrapped up the constructors' championship in the Italian Grand Prix. Standing on the podium at The Glen, and pouring a whole bottle of champagne into the world championship silver bowl, felt so good.

to promote its region and its technology. 'Occasionally, a young Saudi prince would hand me an envelope full of money—$10,000—just to say thank you,' Jones smiled.

Head built a strong, agile car. Compared to the technological marvels of Formula One cars today, it 'was dead simple,' Alan explained. 'There was no power steering, not like today, and downforce and camber made it really heavy, so you had to be fairly strong in the upper body. It had a five-speed gearshift sitting close to the right-hand side of the steering wheel, and you'd use a clutch for every gear change. There was no brake assist—you modulated the braking with your foot.' Jones had a problem with that. 'Every few races I'd get a real pain in the ball of my right foot, usually with about ten laps to go.' There was no treatment for it; he just got on with the job. 'The steering wheel had an ignition switch, an engine kill switch, a talk button'—there was no radio communication between car and pit, but when the car pulled in, the team manager could plug in a cable to talk to his driver—'and a

fluid bottle switch to suck water up from a Ford Transit van windscreen washer bottle.' Jones didn't drink the water: 'I chose not to hydrate during a race.'

Tactics were simple. 'Put your head down and go,' Jones said. 'We figured the tyres would last and we carried enough fuel. Patrick was good at that. He'd calculate fuel mileage exactly. He once ripped into me because I finished with enough fuel for another two laps.' It was rudimentary but effective. 'Daniel Ricciardo drove my car at Paul Ricard recently and he said he couldn't believe how good the brakes are,' Jones said. That car belongs to Zak Brown, now head of McLaren.

Jones climbed the podium once in the 1978 season—second in the US Grand Prix—and finished eleventh in the title. The following year, Frank Williams gave him a teammate, Clay Regazzoni, and Patrick Head gave them both the FW07, Williams' first ground-effects car. Immense aerodynamic downforce was created by the shaped undersides of the car: 'I had to readjust my whole technique,' Jones said. 'It was so much faster.' Or, in terms Jones used so well: 'It stuck like shit to a blanket.'

At the British Grand Prix, Jones claimed a dominant pole position, his first ever in Formula One, and was leading until his engine overheated and Regazzoni won the FW07's first GP. That fired Jones up so much he won the next three grands prix in succession, then another at the end of the season. He finished third in the title and Williams, an F1 afterthought two years before, was second to Ferrari in the constructors' championship. But Williams didn't spray champagne: that was against the beliefs of their Saudi sponsors.

Alan Jones won the Formula One world championship in 1980, doggedly, determinedly, one race at a time. The French F1 press used to give two prizes each year—the Prix Orange to the driver who they judged to be the most approachable, and the Prix Citron to the driver they regarded as the most difficult. Jones won the Orange in 1979 and the Citron in 1980; 1980 was his year of maximum attack. Nothing was going to stand in the way of his single-minded concentration, not even his new teammate Carlos Reutemann. ('He went on to be a politician. He was suited to that.') At a grand prix his attitude was intimidating—one of pure determination. Jones won five grands prix that year, with five fastest laps and three pole positions.

Two grands prix from season's end, Jones and Brazilian Nelson Piquet (Brabham) were both in the running to win the title. They lined up on the front row of the Canadian Grand Prix and collided in the first corner. Jones was accused of slamming the door shut on the Brazilian. His response was that he didn't see Piquet and the corner was his. Most likely, he forced him into the wall. Piquet was compelled to use his spare car at the restart (they had them back then). It was as if Jones had planned it.

The Williams garage knew the second Brabham was a cheater, used to win pole in qualifying with a special high-compression engine on special fuel. Jones won the restart but two laps later Piquet was through, moving away, uncatchable. That was okay. On lap 23, Piquet blew. A special engine was never going to last race distance. Jones won the championship.

Alan Jones is a complex person, volatile (like his dad, a known hothead pugilist) but unemotional. Had there been a microphone in his Williams it's unlikely there would have been the whoops of joy now heard at the end of each grand prix. Forty years on, I asked him: were there tears? 'I had to hold them back,' he admitted, a bit embarrassed. 'I didn't want to get out of the car crying like Bob Hawke.'

Jones rates the next race, the US Grand Prix, as his most enjoyable ever. It was the last grand prix held on the bumpy, elevated Watkins Glen circuit and the championship pressure was off. There's a zone that drivers get into: 'Your body ceases to exist. You are driving simply out of your head, and your arms and legs operate automatically,' Jones explained. He simply blew the field away, won the race and, after his teammate Reutemann punted Piquet off, it was a Williams 1–2.

In 1981, Frank Williams paid Alan Jones $1.2 million (about $3.5 million today). He believes that made him the highest-paid racing driver of the year. He also wrote an ironclad contract that gave Jones precedence over Reutemann. If both cars were comfortably in the lead, Carlos had to yield to Alan. In Brazil, he didn't, and won the race from Jones, second. From Jones' perspective, it was total betrayal and 'all bets were off'.

The last race of the season was the Caesars Palace Grand Prix in Las Vegas. This time Reutemann was challenging Piquet for the title with Jones in third, but

In the deciding race of the 1981 world title, Alan Jones (left) orchestrated a 'confidence trick' that arguably cost his Williams teammate Carlos Reutemann (right) the championship. By the time Reutemann realised he'd been duped, Jones was already in the lead into the first corner of the Caesars Palace Grand Prix and Reutemann was battling for third place (below).

too far back to be in contention unless the other two dropped out. The Williams cars locked out the front row, with Reutemann on pole. Jones was persuasive. He convinced Reutemann that the outside position was fastest and magnanimously offered it to him. Reutemann gratefully accepted. It was total chicanery, a mischief ('Frank could see what I was up to'). Jones bolted from the inside and won the race. Reutemann, demoralised, slipped backwards to eighth and lost the world championship by one point to Piquet. Jones retired from Formula One that day. It was a nice way to leave.

He had offers. 'I was pig-headed, stupid,' Jones told me. 'McLaren called me and asked me to drive at Monaco because Niki had a cold. I didn't go. Ferrari asked me to sub for Didier Pironi at Monza—finally, a Ferrari drive. I refused just to spite them.'

But money brought him back. In 1985, legendary US team owner Carl Haas decided to go Formula One racing with money from massive American food corporation Beatrice. They paid Jones $1.8 million. He ceremonially opened the inaugural Australian F1 Grand Prix in Adelaide in the car and did just three races in 1985. In the entire 1986 season he finished four races, including one place off the podium in Austria, and was twelfth in the title. Then the Beatrice money stopped (the company's chairman was fired by the board while he was attending a motor race at Elkhart Lake) and so did Jones.

His list of victories is illustrious—winner of the 1978 Can-Am Challenge, winner of the 1982 Australian GT Championship, second in the 1993 Australian Touring Car Championship. In 1980, his world-championship year, he brought his Williams Cosworth to Australia and, on the tiny Calder Park circuit, lapped the field to win the Australian Grand Prix—emulating his father.

Alan divorced and remarried. With his wife Amanda, he has twins Jack and Zara. It is Zara's equestrian trophies that are on display in their Gold Coast island home. Long ago, Alan auctioned off his own awards. He recalls they fetched about $10,000. 'Better than Niki,' he said. 'He used to get his car washed and, instead of cash, he paid one trophy a wash.' Alan retained his World Drivers' Championship trophy. It's on display at Motorsport Australia's Hall of Fame in Melbourne.

Alan Jones (Beatrice Lola THL1) was given the honour of running the first practice lap of the new F1 Australian Grand Prix circuit in the Adelaide Parklands in 1985. A year later he retired from the same race in the THL2, and retired from Formula One.

GEOFF'S BOYS
Peter Collins
Peter Windsor

IN 1960, AUSTRALIA'S PREMIER HORSERACING PROMOTER, the Australian Jockey Club (although the Victoria Racing Club might disagree), built the country's finest permanent car-racing facility, a 3.6-kilometre grand prix track weaving around its number-two equine facility at Warwick Farm in Sydney's south-west. It closed just thirteen years later. In that time, it hosted four Australian Grands Prix and ten rounds of the Tasman Series. It brought the world's best grand prix racers to Australia and was the forerunner of the Australian round of the world championship. The AJC hired an Englishman, Geoffrey Percy Frederick Sykes, to run Warwick Farm and provide a springboard for young Australians to race overseas. He instituted Australia's first Driver to Europe program and quietly started a cadetship for young people who might grow to become influential in Formula One. Two of his star graduates were Peter Collins and Peter Windsor.

Peter Windsor was abducted from the darkened car park of Williams F1. Three thugs threw him into a van, drove him to a remote location and beat him severely. He remembers at least one baseball bat. It was a classic London East End cliché. 'I thought I was going to be killed,' Windsor said.

Peter Windsor (right) has had a 40-year association with Formula One and its supremo, Bernie Ecclestone (left). Windsor's attempt to return the Brabham team to its Australian roots after fifteen years of ownership by Ecclestone was unsuccessful. After a series of owners, the Brabham team left the F1 grid in 1992.

It was 1991, and Windsor had been part of a failed bid to buy Brabham F1. 'My original idea had been to buy Lotus,' Windsor said. Windsor had been team manager with Williams, and he'd learned a lot. He was 35 and felt invincible. 'Then Brabham became available.' He thought there would be value in combining two Australian icons and put the concept to golf legend Greg Norman. 'He liked the idea of owning a team.' But the sale became complicated and Norman withdrew. Instead Brabham quickly passed through three sets of hands. 'I was the idiot caught in the middle,' Windsor said. The sale ended up in the law courts and Windsor was ultimately awarded a settlement. But it came at a price. Windsor told me that a while later, a well-known figure in Formula One walked with him, still recovering from the beating, out onto a pier at Monaco. 'It's over now, you know that,' Windsor says he was told.

The Peters—Windsor and Collins—had met at Warwick Farm. Geoff Sykes created the position of personal assistant there, which gave the lads the right to present themselves to any of the visiting teams with missives from the secretary of the meeting's headquarters—'Please, Mr Clark'—their hero—'Mr Sykes wonders if it would be convenient for you to join him in his office.'

Both were eager to get to the UK. Between them, they would work at senior level for seven teams, be involved in the formation or purchase of four teams, have substantial influence in the success of at least one world champion (Nigel Mansell) and, for a time, live precariously on the edge of insolvency.

Peter Windsor became sponsorship manager for Frank Williams' Formula One team. On 8 March 1986, he had just left a test session at the Paul Ricard circuit in the south of France and was being driven by Frank to Nice airport. 'I hadn't done much road driving with Frank, but I was aware a stopwatch was part of his DNA,' Windsor told me from his London home. Williams was a racer in all senses. He was rushing home that Saturday night because he was due to run in a half-marathon in the UK on Sunday morning. 'He was throwing the rental Ford Sierra around, pitching and flicking it through corners with the tail out.' But then the car flipped and came to rest upside down with the roof crushed. Frank called out, 'I'm trapped', but he wasn't. He'd crushed his fourth and fifth vertebrae and had become a permanent tetraplegic. At that moment, Windsor's priority was saving Frank's life.

Windsor travelled with Frank in the bumpy Citroen Deux Chevaux ambulance to Marseilles, called Frank's wife Ginny down from London and sat with them for a week. He liaised with Formula One medical supremo Dr Sid Watkins

Sir Frank Williams was rendered tetraplegic in a road crash in 1986; Peter Windsor (left) was alongside him in the car, heading for Nice. Windsor's sound actions may have saved Sir Frank's life. The Williams team, responsible for nine World Constructors' Championships and seven World Drivers' Championships, was sold in September 2020.

('If we don't get him out of here, he'll die'), and was part of the repatriation effort mounted by Mark Thatcher, son of the British prime minister. Finally, he joined the resistance when there was a push to turn off Williams' life-support system.

Windsor became team manager of Williams Formula One, with Frank, permanently wheelchair bound, then left as part of his restless quest to own a team of his own. It was a passion he shared with Peter Collins.

Peter Collins had his ownership moment in 1990. With colleague Peter Wright, he bought Team Lotus from the Chapman family. When Colin Chapman had died of a heart attack in December 1982, aged 54, the team had struggled. Collins had been close to Chapman and worked with him in several roles.

Only a miracle could have turned Lotus around. Collins and Wright battled for four years but in September 1994 the team applied for administration orders to protect itself from creditors. Its debt was in the region of £12 million (A$25.6 million) and the vultures picked at it. The last race for Team Lotus was the 1994 Australian Grand Prix. Neither car finished.

Clearly, Peter Windsor did not listen the first time; he had a second attempt at team ownership in 2009. Working out of Charlotte, North Carolina—a long way from F1 central—he launched US F1, a bold attempt to capture the financial support of the American market, which had never fully bought into the concept of Formula One. Windsor did a good job, raising finance from investors including Chad Hurley, co-founder of YouTube. But in December 2009, Bernie Ecclestone

Opposite: Peter Collins (right) had dreamed of working with Lotus F1 and with his heroes Colin Chapman (left) and Jim Clark. Clark died in 1968, but Collins became a senior member of Team Lotus, working under Chapman.

Above: Eight years after Colin Chapman suffered his fatal heart attack in 1982, Peter Collins (left) became co-managing director of Lotus F1 with Peter Wright (right). Win or lose, it was the realisation of a lifetime's ambition.

publicly expressed doubts the team would be race-ready in 2010. It was the seed of doubt that Windsor didn't need sown. By February, investors had started to withdraw and by March all team members were made redundant. Mid-year, the FIA's World Motor Sport Council fined US F1 €309,000 (around A$435,000) for failing to fulfil its obligation to start in 2010, and banned it from future FIA-sanctioned events.

Big noise in North Carolina. The former voice of American motor racing, Bob Varsha (left), before Australian Leigh Diffey took over, dialled up the man whose name is synonymous with speed, Mario Andretti, to bring gravitas to the 2009 announcement by Peter Windsor (right) and his partner Ken Anderson (second from right) that their team US F1 would be joining the world championship grid. It didn't.

It's a big call, but Britain's bulldog of a world champion, Nigel Mansell, owes his career to the enthusiasm and persuasion of both Peters. Windsor was working as a journalist, Collins as assistant manager at Lotus.

They truly appreciated Mansell's pace and dogged determination. Windsor and Collins begged Colin Chapman to give Mansell a test. And that launched a twelve-year soap opera before he won his title. He was so unlike other drivers, publicly taking his fans with him on his exciting, excruciating ride. He drove for Lotus, then moved to Williams.

The 1986 Australian Grand Prix—the last round of the year—was looking set to deliver Mansell his world championship; Mansell needed only to finish fourth or better to claim the title. He was in third place when his left rear tyre exploded. He fought the bucking, weaving Williams to a safe standstill from 300 km/h,

Peter Collins (centre) was able to work closely with Nigel Mansell (right), the driver he most admired, first at Lotus and then in 1985 at Williams. Frank Williams (left) gave Mansell his best chance to win the world championship, and finally succeeded with Mansell's second stint with the team in 1992. By then Collins was running Lotus, fielding Mika Häkkinen and Johnny Herbert.

still claiming second in the title. Years later, Mansell suggested that had he not been so skilful and instead had crashed into the wall, the race would have been stopped and he would have become world champion based on his race position at the time of the stoppage.

He went to Ferrari in 1989, returned to Williams two years later and won his championship, finally, for Williams in 1992.

Peter Windsor and Peter Collins remain within motorsport. Collins and his daughter Samantha run Allinsports, a Swiss-based strategic consultancy that concentrates on new driver development. Windsor has become an eminent F1 commentator. He is the proud owner of a half-century-old Lotus Elan sports car, once owned by Jim Clark.

The moment of delamination. Nigel Mansell was topping 300 km/h on Dequetteville Terrace in the 1986 Australian Grand Prix at Adelaide—bound for his world championship—when his tyre exploded and the Williams dropped to the ground. Mansell fought the beast for more than half a kilometre before he stopped, safely, up the escape road.

13

AUSSIE GRIT TAKES ON THE WORLD
Mark Webber
Daniel Ricciardo

IN A PERIOD OF JUST SEVEN YEARS, AUSTRALIANS MARK Webber and Daniel Ricciardo claimed third place in the Formula One world championship five times, both driving for the Red Bull Racing team. By 2020 they had won sixteen grands prix between them, all with Red Bull Racing, and had both taken a celebratory plunge into the pool at Monte Carlo after winning the Monaco Grand Prix.

MARK WEBBER

Dr Helmut Marko, a former Austrian Formula One driver whose own career was cut short when he lost the sight in his left eye in a racing incident, became Mark Webber's bête noire at Red Bull Racing, just when the Australian needed the entire team pulling in his direction to win the world championship. The extraordinary public clash between Webber and Marko (he has a doctorate in law), head of Red

Webber's first ride. In the 2002 Australian Grand Prix, Mark Webber claimed a glorious fifth and scored the only championship points of the season for Paul Stoddart's (left) wooden-spoon European Minardi team. Australian Stoddart had purchased the cash-strapped team the previous year and provided springboard drives for both Webber and Fernando Alonso. Stoddart sold the team to Dietrich Mateschitz in 2005 and it became Scuderia Toro Rosso, later morphing in 2020 into Scuderia AlphaTauri, representing Red Bull's fashion merchandising company.

Mark Webber (right) with two of the people most influential in his F1 career—Dietrich Mateschitz (left), owner of energy drink company Red Bull and the team that bears its name, and (centre) Helmut Marko. Marko has been with Red Bull Racing since its inception in 2005. By the beginning of 2021, he had overseen twelve drivers, 68 grand prix wins and 191 podiums, and the team had become the sixth most successful of all time in F1. Webber was the team's third most successful GP winner.

Bull's junior development program and a major influence within the Formula One team, destabilised and arguably derailed the Aussie's best shot at the title.

The global energy drink company had taken up Formula One as the first of its many extreme sports partnerships. Marko had sold the concept of a junior development squad to owner Dietrich Mateschitz: better to grow its own talent and have a ready pool of replacements in the high-turnover world of modern Formula One.

Marko was old school, a clone of his three-time-world-champion countryman Niki Lauda. Both men eschewed team uniforms, opting for unfashionable, ill-fitting jeans, with shirts spilling over their paunches. It was a statement, and they stood out. They played at being gruff.

But Marko was building champions. Young German driver Sebastian Vettel was his star. Vettel had joined the Red Bull Academy in karts and been promoted to the feeder Formula One team, Scuderia Toro Rosso, at nineteen. Under the control of the safety car in the rain-affected 2007 Japanese Grand Prix he'd hit third-placed Mark Webber in the Red Bull car and cost him the podium: 'It's kids with not enough experience, isn't it. You do a good job and then they fuck it all up,' Webber fumed. Less than a year later, Vettel became the youngest driver at the time to win a grand prix at 21 years, 74 days. It was a spectacular victory. He was promoted to the Red Bull senior team as Webber's teammate.

Marko had a lot riding on Vettel. Three of his junior team's graduates—Christian Klien, Vitantonio Liuzzi and Scott Speed—had already been through the F1 spin cycle without blazing success. But Vettel was the real deal, a grand prix winner and a true protégé, one to prove the efficacy of the junior program. 'He's the man to end Webber's career,' Marko is said to have told the team.

It was the start of a four-year war. When it was over, Webber's Formula One career had concluded.

Alan Webber owned a motorcycle dealership in Queanbeyan and, as a red-hot motor-racing fan, took his young son to everything from the local Canberra speedway, Tralee, to the Australian F1 Grand Prix in Adelaide. He funded a kart, and when Mark won the 1993 NSW Juniors, Alan bought the Formula Ford in which Craig Lowndes had won the 1993 Australian championship. Mark was thirteenth in his first year of the title, fourth in the next. There were people who finished above him who have disappeared from motor racing. So why did Webber succeed when they didn't? The answer is Ann Neal: 'She told me in no uncertain terms that I had to get my ass out of Australia,' Webber said.

Alan Webber had hired Ann, formerly PR manager for Australian Formula Ford, to find sponsorship for Mark. She did more than that—she adopted him as her cause, and that led to a relationship. The decade-plus difference in their ages was a source of titillation at the time, but not so now that they've both matured. They married when his driving career was over.

There's no doubting Webber's raw talent. He was a debut third in the British Formula Ford Festival at Brands Hatch—effectively the Formula Ford world championship. That was a wake-up call for Webber: 'Even when the yellow [warning] flags are out, drivers are still trying to punt each other off.'

In 1996, Webber raced two Formula Ford championships. He was third in the European, second in the British. He signed on with Australian Alan Docking's Formula Three team, and that cost money. Australian Rugby Union's

Team Webber on the day of their first grand prix victory: the 2009 German Grand Prix. Ann Neal, now Ann Webber, had guided Webber's career since he was eighteen. The fifteen intervening years—incorporating junior formulas, a stint with the Mercedes works sports-car team and 130 grands prix for four teams—had been intense. 'This wasn't my day,' Webber said. 'It was ours.'

goose-stepping legend David Campese, a proud lad from Queanbeyan, provided the stake. The rugby pitch in Queanbeyan is named for Campese; the kart track across the border in the ACT is named for Webber. With Campo's money, Webber came fourth in the British Formula Three Championship and was Rookie of the Year.

At 9.57 p.m. on Thursday 10 June 1999, on a steaming hot night, the sun set over Le Mans in north-western France. An afterglow remained as Europe's fastest sports cars practised for that weekend's 24 Hour race. Mark Webber was in the works Mercedes CLR and it went airborne at 300 km/h, completed three mid-air flips and landed on its wheels.

He had been hired the year before as a works Mercedes sports-car driver—a huge boost in the career of a 22-year-old. Mercedes was re-entering motor racing in its own name, the first time since the 1955 Le Mans crash that had killed more than 80 spectators—the worst disaster, ever, in motor racing.

Mercedes didn't believe Webber when he said it just flew and that it was most likely an aerodynamic fault. They held an impromptu conference and said nothing, except they'd referred the crash to their board of directors in Stuttgart. They put more wing on the car, made it safer, but never made a move to withdraw the team, not even after the lessons of '55.

On Saturday morning, in warm-up for the race, it happened again. 'I just could not believe it,' Webber said. This time the car landed on its roof and skidded down the track. The Mercedes, thankfully, was structurally sound and Webber was uninjured. He had survived two near-death experiences. 'Driver error' was the not too subtle wink-and-a-nod given by the Mercedes PR people. They started the race that afternoon, without the concussed Webber. On lap 75, the second of the team's three cars, driven by Scotsman Peter Dumbreck, pitchpoled into the trees. He too was unscathed. Then, and only then, Mercedes called their third car back into the pits and pulled down the shutter doors, perhaps to hide their embarrassment. Mark Webber pledged never to drive a sports car again. It was a promise he'd keep until after he retired from Formula One. Then he went on to win the World Endurance Championship with Porsche.

The Australian F1 Grand Prix has traditionally been the first round of the world championship, so naturally it's the place where F1 debutants come out. In 2002, Webber was in fellow Australian Paul Stoddart's Minardi, in front of his home crowd, and he came fifth. He was in the points at his first attempt. There is a strict protocol in Formula One—only the top three mount the podium.

But after that ceremony was over, the chairman of the Australian Grand Prix Corporation, the late Ron Walker AC, dragged Webber and Stoddart up there, Aussie flags waving, and staged a presentation for fifth. Michael Schumacher, winner of the grand prix, made a point of having his photo taken with Webber, because he knew it was his only hope of being on page one in the Australian papers the next morning.

It had taken Mark and Ann two years to secure that drive. They'd passed through Formula 3000 (Mark was third and second in his European championship seasons), stalked team owner Eddie Jordan (until his chauffeur shook their tail) and signed a management contract with the controversial but incredibly well-connected Flavio Briatore. Mark was appointed test driver for the Arrows F1 team and the Briatore-managed Benetton team.

But his first Formula One race drive was with the team regarded as the wooden-spooner, and he gave Minardi its best result. His connections shuttled him through Jaguar in 2003 and 2004, then Williams for the next two years, each move, on paper, a step up. But all those four years netted him was his first podium—a third at Monaco in 2005.

He had looked forward to his time with Williams. The team was Aussie-friendly. But for Webber it didn't gel. 'We've got you for another year, but if there's a way we don't have to have you that would be fine,' he says team co-owner Patrick Head told him. Worse, Webber had passed up an opportunity to move to Renault. He felt so positively about Williams that he'd baulked at Briatore's suggestion he join the French team. In the two years Webber was at Williams, Briatore's other driver under management, Fernando Alonso, won two world championships at Renault.

In 2005, Ford sold its Jaguar Formula One team to Red Bull to become Red Bull Racing. A year late, Paul Stoddart's Minardi became Red Bull's junior team Scuderia Toro Rosso. When Webber joined Red Bull in 2007, he knew many of the faces in the workshop. He'd worked with them for the bulk of his Formula One career.

According to *Forbes* magazine, Dietrich Mateschitz in 2021 had a net worth of US$26.9 billion and was the 56th-wealthiest person in the world. When he was 38, Mateschitz discovered a sweetened, non-carbonated health drink in Thailand—a cure for his jet lag. He took Krating Daeng, Thai for 'Red Bull', to Europe and made his fortune. It was easy to believe he could deliver on a simple thing like a world championship.

Instead, Webber and David Coulthard, another Williams alumnus, languished for two seasons. Webber claimed his second career podium, a third in the 2007 European Grand Prix and, as their team developed, he spent his time outqualifying Coulthard 34:4. But in 2008 both were beaten in championship points by Scuderia Toro Rosso team leader Sebastian Vettel (he was eighth, Webber eleventh, Coulthard sixteenth). That wasn't supposed to happen. Vettel outqualified them five times and claimed the first grand prix win for the Red Bull brand in the Italian Grand Prix.

In the off-season, Webber had embraced Mateschitz's passion for adventure. He'd launched the high-profile Mark Webber Challenge, a charity race around Tasmania in kayaks, on mountain bikes and on foot. Webber, competing, collided with a four-wheel drive. He broke his leg and shoulder. He walked into Mateschitz's office on crutches, his leg pinned and screwed. Mateschitz didn't need to tell him his teammate for the 2009 season would be Vettel. He was in enough pain already.

It was a sensational battle. The two were evenly matched and their rivalry was intense. When Vettel won in China, Webber was second. Webber was third in Spain, Vettel fourth; Webber second in Turkey, Vettel third. When Vettel won the British Grand Prix, Webber completed a Red Bull 1–2.

In Germany, Webber scored his first ever grand prix victory. Vettel was second.

Webber's win came after a record 130 grands prix without a victory—a record he held until Sergio Pérez won on his 190th attempt in 2020. Webber's on-air exaltation, straight from the helmet to the TV audience, was one of the longest and least contrived in the modern history of Formula One entertainment.

He backed it up with a win in the penultimate grand prix of the season in Brazil. Jenson Button won the world championship in Ross Brawn's Mercedes-powered, Honda-built car. Vettel was second and Webber fourth. For the next four years, the title would be Red Bull's.

According to Webber, a journalist walked into Red Bull's garage after his German GP win and asked: 'Why the long faces?' And then said: 'I see—the wrong driver won.' Modern F1 team dynamics are complex. Webber has a dossier of resentments that he holds against Dr Helmut Marko. Life within the Red Bull team had increasingly become Team Webber (Mark and Ann) vs Team Red Bull.

And yet Red Bull yielded so much for Webber—two victories in the Monaco Grand Prix, two British Grands Prix, nine grand prix victories in total, and more visits to the podium (42) than any other Australian, including Jack Brabham (31).

Mark Webber's resounding 9.25-second victory over teammate Sebastian Vettel in the 2009 German Grand Prix set up a chain of podium finishes over the next four seasons, with sufficient wins to net him three third places in the world championship—in 2010, 2011 and 2013. Webber featured strongly in one of the most competitive eras of the world title.

In 2010, he could have been world champion. He lost that opportunity when he spun on an incredibly greasy track in South Korea. That cost him, potentially, 25 points. In Brazil he was told to hold station behind Vettel even though he was leading the championship. That cost him another seven points. And then in the final winner-takes-all race in Abu Dhabi he was boxed in behind Fernando Alonso's Ferrari and finished eighth while Vettel sprinted off to win the race and the title. Webber was third in the championship, fourteen points behind his young teammate. 'The only time Seb led the championship all year was at the chequered flag of the final race,' Webber wryly noted.

Vettel won the next three world championships in succession and Webber's disgruntlement was increasingly on display. In 2010, when he won his first British Grand Prix—a massive accomplishment—he punctuated it with a pithy remark from the cockpit: 'Not bad for a number-two driver.' He flirted with Ferrari, but halfway through 2012 he signed up with Red Bull again; the money was too good to refuse.

Before the start of that last season, Helmut Marko caused Team Webber public offence. In an op-ed in Red Bull's own well-read magazine *The Red Bulletin*, he wrote: 'It seems to me that Webber has on average two races per year where he is unbeatable, but he can't maintain this form throughout the year. And as soon as his prospects start to look good in the world championship, he has a little trouble with the pressure that this creates.' He went on to unfavourably compare Webber with Vettel. It was too much: 'The man was now persona non grata,' Webber said, 'and I don't think we ever spoke to him again.'

In 2013, the entire horrible, dysfunctional relationship went on display at the Malaysian Grand Prix. 'Multi-21', the teammates were told towards the end of the race while Webber was leading, and Vettel was second. It was team code, and it directed the drivers to hold station. Vettel disobeyed, muscled past Webber and won the race. Afterwards he apologised, although he was most likely unrepentant. Webber claims that Red Bull later received a letter from Vettel's lawyer alleging they'd been in breach of his contract by giving him an unreasonable team order. In the modern world of Formula One, such an action is entirely plausible.

In 2014, Webber did not renew with Red Bull Racing and retired from Formula One. 'I can honestly say that we'd been beaten by a power structure,' he said in his autobiography (of late he's loath to discuss it). 'Nothing was ever going to change in Red Bull Racing.' But: 'I can say with absolute honesty that Sebastian was a better all-round Formula One driver than I ever was. I suspected that he was just as much a pawn in the game as I had been.'

Webber and Neal had an ace up their sleeve. They'd negotiated an association with Porsche. Mark anchored the Porsche World Endurance Championship team for three years, driving the most technologically advanced cars in the world—more so even than Formula One—and in 2015, along with teammates Timo Bernhard and Brendon Hartley, he became world champion.

En route to victory, he survived a massive crash, his worst ever, in the final round of the 2014 series at São Paulo in Brazil. His car was destroyed; Webber escaped with bruising. 'I was a lucky boy,' he said. He could well have been talking about his career.

DANIEL RICCIARDO

Daniel Ricciardo replaced Mark Webber at Red Bull Racing in 2014 and blew Sebastian Vettel away.

His first race was the 2014 Australian F1 Grand Prix. He muscled his way to second place behind Nico Rosberg, bounded onto the podium and gave Victorian premier Denis Napthine a huge hug. He was the first Australian ever on the podium in his home world championship grand prix.

Hours later, stewards took it away. For the first time, Formula One cars were using on-board fuel-flow meters to ensure they did not exceed the allowed maximum of 100 kilograms of fuel per hour. Only Ricciardo's Red Bull was found to be in contravention of regulation.

Monaco Grand Prix celebrations. Red Bull Racing built its own rooftop swimming pool above its VIP hospitality area in Monte Carlo. Mark Webber (above) celebrated his 2012 victory with a technically competent backward somersault. Daniel Ricciardo (opposite) was more of a classicist. His 2018 swan dive had all the poise of a proud son of Western Australia with the swan as its state emblem.

Daniel was no novice. He'd been with Scuderia Toro Rosso since 2012, but when he was promoted to the senior squad in 2014, he lifted his game to another level. He outqualified Vettel 11:9 (that was close), and outfinished him 15:4 (not so close). When the championship points were tallied, Ricciardo was third and Vettel was fifth.

On the Friday night of the 2014 Japanese Grand Prix, with five races to go in the season, Vettel summoned Red Bull team management to his hotel room and told them he would be leaving at the end of the year. He had accepted a seat with Ferrari, replacing Fernando Alonso. The proclamation blindsided Red Bull. 'I'm not running away and it's nothing against Red Bull,' Vettel told the media. 'There are times in your life when you need to start something new.' Vettel had

been with Red Bull for sixteen years. It was the only racing life he knew. Team boss Christian Horner had no choice but to accept: 'If someone's heart is not there it doesn't matter what you have on a piece of paper.'

That year was the beginning of Mercedes-AMG's near-decade of dominance of the sport. Ricciardo finished the season behind the two Mercedes-AMG Silver Arrows, and even if his result in Melbourne had stood, it wouldn't have changed his position.

Daniel Ricciardo, Australia's great Formula One hope, is proudly claimed by the Sicilian region of Ficarra as one of its two favourite sons (they have only two)—even though he wasn't born there.

'When I was about five, my grandfather put me on his shoulders and took me down to watch racing cars rushing through the roads of northern Sicily. It could have been the Targa Florio, but I'm not sure,' said Giuseppe 'Joe' Ricciardo, Daniel's dad, as he explained the family heritage and his own incredible dedication to the sport that became Daniel's life. The Ricciardo family were citizens of Ficarra, but Joe's mum and dad, Josephine and Francesco, sailed away with their seven-year-old son in search of a better life. They landed in Perth.

At his very first Australian school, Giuseppe became 'Joe' and his surname, pronounced 'Ri-chee-ardo' in Italian, became 'Rick-ardo'. Joe loved cars. 'My passion was pre-war Auto Unions,' he said, but he settled for a V8 Ford Anglia sports sedan built by former Formula One engineer Bruce Carey. It fired his passion. In 1977, 24-year-old Joe Ricciardo joined the exodus of young hopefuls seeking their motor-racing fortune in Great Britain. 'I arrived at the Jim Russell Racing School and told them I was the best. They were most accommodating. They asked me which championship I'd like to do—Formula Ford, Formula Three—then they gave me a price list: £12,000 [A$20,000] for a Formula Ford test, £18,000 [A$30,000] for a Formula Three. I settled for a job in the workshop.'

Joe worked with hopefuls like the precocious New Zealander Mike Thackwell. He hooked up with fellow Western Australian Barry Green, who went on to

Danny Ric's point of difference: a Cheshire cat grin and his incredibly enthusiastic parents Grace and Joe, here at the 2018 Monaco Grand Prix. Ricciardo's personality sets him apart from the Formula One grid. No one smiles like Daniel—even, it seems, in the face of great adversity. 'If the team is a bit down after a poor result, I'm the one who tries to lift it,' he says. 'The smile is never fake.'

IndyCar success. 'I was in the European paddock with Gilles Villeneuve and Nigel Mansell, and I did get to do some Jim Russell club races, all while earning £40 [A$65] a week.' Joe was living the dream.

Then his dad called: 'If you don't get a job, you'll be sleeping in the park.' Joe returned to Australia and bought 'a heap-of-shit wheel loader' and built that one piece of machinery into a sizeable fleet. 'I did it for one purpose only,' Joe said. 'So I could go motor racing.'

Joe is not exactly a household name, but he has raced in national open-wheeler and sports-sedan championships. His stable of racing cars includes a McLaren M10B F5000, a Schenken and Ganley Tiga, a genuine Alfa Romeo GTA, and other highly collectible road cars that he prefers to keep secret. In England, during Daniel's formative Formula One years, he owned a classic HWM-Alta Formula One car to race at Goodwood, and he is quick to point out its connection to Australia's first world championship contender Tony Gaze.

Joe is a gold-standard enthusiast. He met his wife Grace, Daniel's mother, at a fundraiser he was holding in Perth in 1984 to support his motor-racing habit.

'I never wanted Daniel to go motor racing,' Joe said. Yeah, sure. 'I would have liked him to be a tennis player. I knew how hard motor racing is, and how much money you need.' The way Joe tells it, young Daniel persisted, and the family invested $700 in a kart 'to get it out of his system'. They took the ten-year-old to the Cockburn track in Perth to race with the Tiger Kart Club. On a wet day, on slick tyres, he decimated a field of karts on grooved wets: 'We were lifting our kart on its trolley by the time the guy in second crossed the line.'

That led to Formula Ford and Daniel came eighth in the Western Australian championship driving a car that was as old as he was. In Southeast Asia, the global Formula BMW series, with a wings-and-slicks car using a 1200cc motorcycle engine, was in full swing, searching for the stars of tomorrow. Its early graduates include Sebastian Vettel and Nico Rosberg. There was a test session in Bahrain that cost A$5000 to enter. 'I left it with Daniel, then fifteen, to sort that out with his mum. I didn't want her to blame me. She had a few tears but then said, "If you want to do it, go."'

Daniel won a scholarship to race in the Asian version of the series out of Malaysia. 'It's a six-hour flight and each time I went with him,' Joe said. 'He scored two wins, came third in the championship and was invited to the UK for the world final. He finished fifth.'

Joe spent $30,000 for Daniel to test a Formula Renault in Spain. 'They gave us a poor engine and I said to the team principal, "What are you doing to us?"

He responded: "We're doing you a favour getting you in at the last minute and besides, he only came third in Asia—it's not like he won." Three laps in he's come to me and said: "Joe, Joe, look what he's doing. He's driving out of the box. People are looking at his data."' Joe could well qualify as the proudest father in motorsport.

'Daniel was an unknown but suddenly people were coming to us, wanting him to drive for their team.' The teams chasing him still wanted money—'around €220,000 [A$355,000] for a season,' Joe said.

The Ricciardos moved to Europe, based themselves at Viareggio on the Tuscan coast in Italy, and supported Daniel through two seasons of Formula Renault. In 2008, he won the Formula Renault 2.0 West European Cup, and was second to Valtteri Bottas in the Eurocup. 'Then he got an email from Red Bull asking him to put himself forward as a candidate for their program,' Joe said. The test was at Estoril in Portugal and Joe went along. 'Later, when he was in Formula One, I asked Helmut Marko what he saw in him,' Joe said. 'Marko said: "He was crazy, out of control, brilliant on cold tyres. I just had to have him."'

Red Bull was, according to Joe, 'our saviour. We still had to pay for his expenses, but the racing was on them.' Red Bull cycled Ricciardo through several championships. In 2009, he became the first Australian since David Brabham to win the British F3 title. The family bought a house in Woburn Sands, Milton Keynes, near the Red Bull factory and 'just down the road from Sir Jackie Stewart'. They sold up and moved back to Western Australia only when Daniel went up to Formula One.

'Red Bull paid €2.5 million [A$3.2 million] for Daniel's first half-season with the Spanish HRT team,' Joe said. It was 2011, off the back of the grid just to give him experience. The next year he joined Scuderia Toro Rosso.

Personality means a lot. The world knows when Daniel Ricciardo has won a race. His smile fills the podium, and he drinks victory champagne from his shoe—he calls it a 'shoey', with a passing nod to Michael Schumacher. He proudly races the number 3 in honour of the great Dale Earnhardt, who died in the Daytona 500 in 2001. Daniel has adopted the persona of the honey badger—'adorable but fierce', a survivor.

His teams love him and support him. Even when his young Russian teammate Daniil Kvyat beat him in the 2015 championship, it was Kvyat who was demoted to the junior team to make way for prodigy Max Verstappen.

Verstappen needed Ricciardo. The Dutchman's crash-through attitude enraged competitors, brought official sanction raining down on his head and led his team

Ricciardo invented the 'shoey', turning his race boot into a champagne flute on the podium. 'At the time I thought, "I'm an idiot for doing this,"' he admitted. 'But it wasn't forced. I wasn't trying to be the class clown. It's just me.'

boss Christian Horner to suggest 'he needs to learn from his teammate'. But the Red Bull pendulum was swinging towards Verstappen.

In the 2018 Azerbaijan Grand Prix, both were eliminated. Max had got ahead at a pit stop and Ricciardo expected that to be redressed by the team. Instead, he was told: 'You are racing Max,' which meant no team orders. Down the straight, Daniel 'sold him the dummy so there was enough room originally on the inside and then he closed it and then we crashed'. It was at that point, according to Joe, that Ricciardo contemplated a change of team.

Two races later, he drove arguably the race of his career. He won the Monaco Grand Prix nursing a failing car that was 25 per cent down on power and had two fewer gears available. It was a masterful effort, a vindication of his ability.

In August, he announced his move in 2019 to Renault, which he would clearly lead. A factory team backed by corporate dollars is every driver's aspiration. There

was huge salary speculation: A\$70 million over two years was one estimate, neither confirmed nor denied by the Ricciardo family. 'I felt it was time when it was good to move on,' Daniel said when leaving Red Bull—a statement very similar to that of Vettel's four years before. (Perhaps the same PR company wrote it.)

But it didn't work. 'We let him down,' Australian Chris Dyer, head of Renault's vehicle performance group, told me. For a start, Renault couldn't muster the firepower, and also it's just possible that the corporate world did not suit Ricciardo's free spirit. Honey badgers don't flourish in captivity.

In 2020, with a full year to go on his Renault contract, Ricciardo signed with McLaren and made the announcement mid-season. He'd developed a rapport with Zak Brown, the can-do American CEO of McLaren. Although McLaren had long ceased to be a New Zealand company, there was a spiritual alliance. An Aussie in Bruce's team with such dedicated heritage had a certain appeal. 'I actually bought a McLaren sports car while I was still with Red Bull,' Ricciardo revealed cheekily.

Ricciardo was 31 and his biological clock was ticking. No one over 30 had been a first-time winner of the world championship since Damon Hill in 1996. The boy wonders—Schumacher, Alonso, Hamilton, Vettel—had all won for the first time in their twenties, but Alan Jones had been 34; Jack Brabham, 33; and Denny Hulme, 31. For those with faith, there was still time.

One of those who believed most strongly was Helmut Marko. 'He is one of the fastest drivers,' Marko told *Motor Sport Magazine* in Ricciardo's last year with the team. Ricciardo had achieved what few others in the Red Bull team had. He'd learned how to stand up to the doctor, goading him jibe for jibe, even wagering a tattoo against race victory. 'It was more fun with Ricciardo,' Marko told Grand Prix.com, a bit wistfully in 2020. 'He looked for his own way, but we are still good friends.'

14

FROM ONE LAP TO ONE SEASON
Warwick Brown
Paul England
Brendon Hartley
Graham McRae
John Nicholson
Tony Shelly
Mike Thackwell

'THE MOST IMPORTANT THING IN THE OLYMPIC GAMES IS not to win but to take part.' The father of the modern Olympic Games, Baron de Coubertin, wrote the Olympic creed. There wouldn't be a Formula One driver in the world who'd agree. They have always been there to win. The truth is, though,

Naked and exposed: Warwick Brown in the tub of his Wolf-Williams FW05 waiting to practise for the 1976 US Grand Prix. The FW05 was a derivation of the Hesketh 308C driven by James Hunt in 1975. Both versions were designed by Dr Harvey Postlethwaite, who went on to pen two World Constructors' Championship-winning Ferraris. Brown barely fitted into the aluminium monocoque tub and was unimpressed with the comparatively heavy car's performance.

that many do not. But by taking the starting flag—or, more recently seeing the starting lights go out—they've earned the right to be recognised as Formula One drivers, the highest calling in motor racing.

WARWICK BROWN

Warwick Brown got off to a rocky start in the 1976 US Grand Prix when he crashed the Wolf-Williams team's rental car on the night before practice with technical chief Patrick Head on board. 'It was 10 p.m., snowing, and we hit black ice and slipped off into the trees. I gave it full opposite lock—just not enough,' smiled Brown, winner of the Australian and New Zealand grands prix and three-time Tasman Series champion. Brown was racing F5000 in the States when he'd got a last-minute call-up from Frank Williams. 'Chris Amon had suffered a severe knee injury on the warm-up lap of the Canadian Grand Prix the week before,

Warwick Brown's Wolf-Williams was as fast in a straight line as current Formula One cars, but with its still-developing technology—both in aerodynamics and mechanical grip—it was slower and less predictable in brakes and cornering. Formula One circuits were struggling to initiate new safety measures. Brown used several layers of 'catch fencing' (behind his car) to restrain his speed when he crashed in practice.

and they needed me. I always said I'd never do F1 unless it was a really good car, but I instantly said yes.'

Brown was underwhelmed. 'I'd been to Watkins Glen six weeks before in the F5000 car and the time I did in that would have put me on the second row of the grid for the F1 race. I couldn't keep the F1 car in a straight line—it was driving me, rather than the other way around.' Brown said the team continued to fly in new suspension components. 'I started to think, "I'll be lucky to live through this."'

Brown was the bravest of the brave. In qualifying, he hit the chicane and launched himself through three rows of catch fence. 'Unfortunately, the photo turned up in the Sydney papers the next day and I'd forgotten to tell my mother I was racing.' Brown qualified 23rd, still in front of his teammate Arturo Merzario, and forced his way up to fourteenth in the race while the little Italian crashed. 'It was the best result they got in the second half of the season,' Brown said. There were promises of a spot in the Japanese Grand Prix, the next and final race of the 1976 season—the rain-soaked event in which James Hunt won the world title from Niki Lauda. 'They kept saying, "If you go to Japan . . ." but there was no firm offer.' Ultimately, the struggling team accepted a Japanese pay driver, Masami Kuwashima, who failed to qualify. Brown wasn't in Japan, so he missed his second F1 drive.

Paul England (Cooper Climax) dives over the rise and into the Karussell, the 210-degree, concrete-faced berm corner on the Nürburgring, in 1957. It wasn't a steep banking and not particularly high-g, but the rough surface severely jarred the drivers' hands and wrists. It was also unsighted. Juan Manuel Fangio, who won the German Grand Prix in which England drove, advised: 'Aim for the tallest tree.'

PAUL ENGLAND

Paul England drove in five-time world champion Juan Manuel Fangio's greatest race. In the 1957 German Grand Prix, Fangio (Maserati 250F) re-broke the Nürburgring's lap record nine times in ten laps to win from behind. 'I have never driven that quickly in my life and I will never do it again,' the Maestro said. Paul England had retired on lap four and watched the whole drama unfold.

An apprentice engineer for Repco in Melbourne, and later three-time winner of the Australian Hill Climb Championship, England went Continental racing in 1957 at the age of 28. He bought a Formula Two Cooper Climax T41 from the estate of the late Ken Wharton, killed that January when his Ferrari Monza flipped in a sports-car race supporting the New Zealand Grand Prix. It was important to be a little pretentious to achieve starting money in Europe, so England formed the Colonial Equipe team and travelled with friends from Kiwi Equipe—Ronnie Moore, who'd later become twice world speedway champion in the British League, and Ray Thackwell. They were good midfield runners and lived on starting money and the occasional prize purse. Initially Moore and Thackwell had the ascendancy but in July 1957 at Reims, on the blazingly fast 8.3-kilometre road course over 307 kilometres, England claimed eighth in the F2 event, with Moore thirteenth. It had been a horrible race. Two drivers were killed in separate crashes.

Organisers of the German F1 Grand Prix were at Reims. They'd opened their field to Formula Two cars. England took up the offer. It would be his first and only F1 world championship race. Three weeks later he lapped the Nürburgring's Eifel circuit in 11 minutes 8.4 seconds to secure 23rd grid position—he'd qualified, and that was an achievement in itself. Fangio on pole did 9 minutes 25.6 seconds. Jack Brabham, in the works F2 Cooper, split the difference: 10 minutes 18.8 seconds.

England raced for 90 kilometres before his Cooper broke down. Brabham joined him in retirement two laps later.

They were able to watch Fangio emphatically claim his 24th and last career victory, and his fifth world title.

BRENDON HARTLEY

Brendon Hartley, twice World Endurance Champion and twice Le Mans 24 Hour winner, faced the dilemma every racer wished they had. In late 2017, he was about to sign an IndyCar contract with Chip Ganassi, one of the best Indy teams of all, when his old nemesis Dr Helmut Marko offered a Red Bull F1 ride. 'His goal had always been F1,' his racer father Bryan said from the family's high-performance race shop in Auckland. 'He had to go for it.'

Brendon had been there once before. In 2012, he had been a promising member of the Red Bull Junior Team but 'they had too many drivers and Brendon was surplus,' Bryan explained. They cut him loose. 'It was pretty harsh.' Now he was back. He did the full 2018 season in F1. Then Red Bull sacked him again.

What could have been: at the end of pre-season testing at Barcelona in 2018, Brendon Hartley (foreground) and his teammate Pierre Gasly unveiled the Toro Rosso STR13, powered for the first time by Honda. The season was mechanically plagued and not successful. Scuderia Toro Rosso was ninth in the constructors' title, its worst result in eight years, and Hartley was released from his contract. Gasly survived the team restructure and in 2020 won the Italian Grand Prix.

Hartley, from a strong motor-racing family, owed his start in Europe to a group of NZ motorsport enthusiasts who delight in supporting young hopefuls. They helped six-time IndyCar champion Scott Dixon, and when Dixon repaid them they invested in Brendon. They got him to Europe when he was sixteen. Within two years he was test and reserve driver for Red Bull.

But instead of progressing, he was dismissed. It was a huge blow, but the NZ support team got behind him again. By 2014, he'd been hired by Porsche for their world sports-car program and in 2017 he won the Le Mans 24 Hour, right before Porsche announced its withdrawal. Hartley's backers suggested he call Dr Marko.

He pumped himself up, made the call, left a message. When Marko called back, his heart rate elevated, just seeing his number come up; he felt like a teenager again: 'There was never really a good call from Helmut.' 'Just give me an opportunity,' he asked Marko. 'At least a day in the sim, a test.' Amazingly, he was in.

He drove for Scuderia Toro Rosso in the last four rounds of the 2017 championship, then did the full 2018 season, 25 starts in all, and earned four career points, 25 behind his teammate Pierre Gasly. By Monaco, early in the season, there was already talk of him being replaced: 'There were some people who didn't want me there,' he told his dad. 'It was a bit of a shock.' And in the end, he was gone. One of the most technically adept drivers of the modern era accepted a role with Toyota in its high-tech LMP1 sports car. In 2020, with Sébastien Buemi and Kazuki Nakajima, Hartley won his second Le Mans 24 Hour race.

GRAHAM MCRAE

Graham McRae, engineer and driver, three-time winner of the Australian Grand Prix, winner of three consecutive Tasman Series, winner of the 1972 US F5000 title, has the shortest Formula One career on record among Australians and New Zealanders. It lasted just 4.711 kilometres, one lap of the Silverstone grand prix circuit. A sticking throttle slide most likely saved him from direct involvement in a first-lap crash that eliminated eleven cars in the 1973 British Grand Prix. When the race resumed, McRae didn't.

Graham McRae's one lap of Formula One competition, in the 1973 British Grand Prix, ended when his throttle slides stuck. McRae was driving the Iso-Marlboro IR (named for Iso Rivolta, the Italian supercar manufacturer), built by Frank Williams (standing at right). Later that season, Australian Tim Schenken placed fourteenth in the car in the Canadian Grand Prix.

McRae was driving for Frank Williams' Iso-Marlboro outfit, the latest in a rotation of racers to become teammates to Howden Ganley, the only constant in the team (Ganley had brought the tobacco company money). The chassis was poor, and Williams called on McRae's analytical skills in another attempt to improve it. McRae was at the top of his game. He had just won Rookie of the Year at the Indianapolis 500 and was the winner also of that year's Australian Grand Prix in a car of his own design. He was, to say the least, self-assured. His competitors called him Cassius (for boxer Cassius Clay—'I am the greatest').

His inclusion in the Williams team was controversial—at least from Ganley's perspective. Williams took McRae testing before the British Grand Prix and left Ganley behind. 'I was told Graham had done so many miles at the test that my spare engine would have to go in his car for practice and the race,' Ganley said. 'Smoke was starting to come out of my ears and as far as I was concerned, there was no way Graham was going to be quicker than me.' Ganley qualified 18th; McRae was 28th. Ganley avoided the first-lap crash and finished ninth.

There could have been a Formula One career waiting for McRae, but he was already 32, arguably too old, and he was tetchy. In 1972, Tyrell had been unable to come to terms with him as a replacement for an ill Jackie Stewart in the Belgian Grand Prix. McRae was most comfortable as a loner and seemed to have a special talent for persuading people not to take the next step with him.

Of late, he is in an Auckland nursing home. After an altercation some 20 years ago, when he used a crossbow to threaten a rock band practising noisily in an industrial complex near his workshop, he was incarcerated, then spent some time sleeping rough before people who admire him found him shelter.

JOHN NICHOLSON

John Nicholson won the 1974 John Player British Formula Atlantic Championship on the same day that Emerson Fittipaldi clinched the Formula One world championship using the engine Nicholson had built. The laidback Auckland-born engineer (he topped the country's technical college exams in his apprentice year) wasn't sure which he should be most excited about, so he accepted both with equanimity. It was also his 33rd birthday.

Nicholson was one of McLaren's Kiwi mafia. He arrived at the factory in 1969, a veteran of the 1968 New Zealand Grand Prix in which he'd finished ninth. Bruce gave him a job working on his V8 Can-Am engines and sent him to the US to head up its new engine division.

When Bruce was killed in 1970, Nicholson returned and commissioned a small chassis maker, Lyncar, to build him a Formula Atlantic car—he won the

John Nicholson was classified seventeenth in the 1975 British Grand Prix, although his own lap chart claimed eleventh. In that year's BRDC International Trophy, a non-championship event, Nicholson (Lyncar 006, #50) raced wheel to wheel with Tony Trimmer (Safir Ford, #52) and Lella Lombardi (March 751, #10). Lombardi led the two men home, nose to tail, in twelfth, thirteenth and fourteenth; that same year she became the first and only woman so far to claim world championship driver's points.

championship in two successive years—then a Formula One car. He had big plans for a driving career.

But when engine maker Cosworth decided not to continue servicing its Formula One engines, opportunity opened. Nicholson went into partnership with McLaren Motors to form Nicholson McLaren, rebuilding DFV engines for much of the Formula One field. The time-poor Nicholson only ever managed to enter two Formula One races, both the British Grand Prix.

He failed to qualify in 1974 and started in last place for the 1975 race. A ferocious hailstorm at three-quarter distance wiped out most of the field, including Nicholson, and he was classified seventeenth when the grand prix was red-flagged. 'It was one of the most boring races I'd done,' he said. 'Just going around with no one nearby to race—but then you find your CV says you've been a grand prix driver.'

Nicholson McLaren still exists today. John Nicholson died in 2017.

TONY SHELLY

Tony Shelly, son of a wealthy Wellington automotive dealer, later with dealerships in Hawaii, was the living example of the gap between amateur and professional motor racing. He did one season in Europe in 1962 and in non-championship races he enthusiastically and skilfully held his own. But when he stepped up to the world championship, he failed to qualify in two out of three attempts. In the British Grand Prix at Aintree, he qualified eighteenth of 21 starters and retired on lap six, with his tired four-cylinder engine overheating. Shelly installed a BRM V8 in a Lotus 24 for the Italian Grand Prix at super-fast Monza but all it did was make him the fastest of the non-qualifiers.

The enthusiastic Shelly raced the 1964 Tasman Series in New Zealand and Australia without claiming a podium position and raced spasmodically while building his business. He died of cancer, aged 61, in 1998.

In 1962, Tony Shelly (left) wore the coveted number 1 on his Lotus Climax in the non-championship International 2000 Guineas race at Mallory Park, UK, after world champion Phil Hill, who was entitled to the number, withdrew his entry. Shelly drove to eighth place, three laps behind second-placed Jack Brabham, shown here passing Shelly in his own Lotus Climax (#8), the car Jack used as an interim between his Cooper and Brabham mounts.

MIKE THACKWELL

Mike Thackwell, aged nineteen years and 182 days, became the youngest driver of his time to start a Formula One grand prix when he raced for Tyrrell in Canada in 1980. The good-looking, blond-haired New Zealander was the hit of European motor racing, touted as a superstar of the future. He was a candle so incandescent he could only flame out. 'It was the vanity, self-obsession, elitism and lack of humbleness that drove me from the sport,' he told *Motor Sport* in 2020. He was racing a sports car in 1987, three years after his F1 career had ended, when he decided, 'That's it'. In 2021, at 60, he is an enigma. People think of him as a Howard Hughes–like figure—a recluse.

'I pushed him into the sport,' his father Ray told me. Ray, 88, lives in Perth, services three mining leases and lives for tomorrow. He was an early mechanic

Mike Thackwell was a serious talent. In the 1980 Dutch Grand Prix he stepped into this Arrows Ford (opposite) at the very last minute as a substitute for its injured driver, Jochen Mass. He was unprepared and 1.3 seconds slower than teammate Riccardo Patrese, failing to qualify. Had he made the field, he would have been the youngest ever driver at the time to start in a grand prix. Instead he had to wait until Canada, later in the year.

for the Cooper Car Company, worked with Jack Brabham, raced on the Continent and wanted something similar for his kids. Daughter Lisa raced saloon cars in the UK and married David Brabham. Mike raced dirt bikes from age six and was third in the 1978 British Formula Ford Championship when he was eighteen. He was dynamic but undirected. Formula One teams wanted a piece of him—too early, because his skills were still developing. His career lacked balance. He won the European Formula Two Championship for RALT four years after he debuted in F1 for Tyrrell. By any measure it was the wrong way around. When a testing crash shattered his heels there was a whole year when teams stayed clear of him.

Ultimately, four teams entered him in just five grands prix. He failed to finish two Canadian grands prix, in 1980 and 1984, and he never saw a chequered flag. It was such a waste—a real talent underdone.

15

SO CLOSE
Bruce Allison
Ryan Briscoe
James Courtney
Will Power
Will Davison
Scott Dixon
Ken Kavanagh
Keith Campbell

THE SUCCESS RATE FOR AUSTRALIANS AND NEW Zealanders achieving their Formula One ambition is surprisingly high. For each driver who has advanced to the Formula One grid, perhaps only one other has tried. Fewer than 60 have set out on the F1 path; 24 have been successful. Of those who returned home without securing a F1 seat, two—John Leffler (1976) and Joey Mawson (2021)—later claimed the Australian Gold Star Championship, an indication both of their talent and of the intense level of competition in F1. A handful of drivers teetered on the brink of a Formula One career, but never made it to the grid.

Will Davison (left) and Will Power (right) taste-tested Formula One on the same day in 2004, driving Australian Paul Stoddart's Minardi PS04B.

BRUCE ALLISON

Bruce Allison, an energetic and, in his day, extremely fast F5000 driver, talked himself out of becoming a world F1 championship contender—twice.

In 1977, Allison's father, 'Big Col', a larger-than-life Queenslander, bought Bruce the ex-Peter Gethin Team VDS Chevron B37 that was second to Warwick Brown in the Australian Grand Prix, gave him an airfare and a grubstake, and sent him off to England to seek his fortune. Bruce repaid him by winning the prestigious Grovewood Motor Racing Award, an annual recognition given to the most promising young driver from Britain and the Commonwealth. He joined a host of previous Australasian winners—Tim Schenken (1968), Vern Schuppan (1971), David Walker (1972), Alan Jones (1974) and Larry Perkins (1975)—and he was followed in 1978 by Mike Thackwell.

On the strength of the Grovewood, 24-year-old Allison got a phone call from John Surtees inviting him to test for the following year's world championship. 'I was living with Alan and Bev Jones in Highgate,' Allison recalled, 'and Alan told me, "Under no circumstances do you want to waste your time." So, I told John Surtees: "No."'

Allison found a ride with RAM Racing, owned by car dealer John Macdonald: 'All I had to do was pay my own expenses.' RAM had big world-championship plans, but in 1978 they were chasing the British F1 Championship, a domestic series. Allison's car was a purpose-built March 781, a Formula Two tub with a Formula One Ford DFV V8—a real rocket. When the car stayed together, he won the Mallory Park round, secured three podiums and claimed sixth in the series.

At season's end, Allison fell out with RAM. 'I was offered a place with another team with a pair of Lotus 78s, but John pointed out he had a contract with me and if I went elsewhere, he'd sue. So, I decided it was all too hard—and quit, walked away from it all.' Macdonald and RAM went on to contest 65 world championship grands prix. 'It could have been me,' said Allison. 'Would I do it differently with my time over? You bet I would.'

Of all the Australian and New Zealand drivers who tried to make it into the F1 World championship, Bruce Allison was the only one to win a Formula One race—the non-championship round of the British F1 series in 1978. He could have been a world title contender. Instead, he made poor choices and gave up his quest too easily. Here Allison (right) stands with RAM team owner John Macdonald (left), alongside teammate Guy Edwards in the RAM Formula One start-up.

RYAN BRISCOE

Ryan Briscoe, a Sydney-born champion kart racer, was trained by the world's best-funded Formula One team to become a world champion. When Toyota decided to go F1 racing in 1999, they talent-scouted eighteen-year-old Briscoe from Italian karting and put him on a seven-year contract to be their great F1 hope. They sent him to school, taught him foreign languages and how to engage with the media. They placed him with sports physician Dr Riccardo Cicarelli at Viareggio who took over development of his still-maturing physique to suit the demands of F1. And they spent millions, entering him in the right feeder series. He won the 2001 Italian Formula Renault Championship and the 2003 Formula Three Euro Series.

Toyota made him their test driver and by the last half of the 2004 season he was 'third driver', driving the team's test car on the Friday of grands prix. But then they let him go.

Toyota was in turmoil. They weren't getting the results their Japanese board expected and they changed direction, hiring experienced name drivers who they hoped would carry their underperforming car and team to victory—unsuccessfully, as it turned out. Ryan called his dad in Australia: 'I'm contemplating going to the States.' Geoff was aghast: 'Not the ovals . . . the ovals are dangerous.' He was right.

Briscoe survived a horrendous, fiery crash at Chicagoland in 2005 but forged a strong Indy career, with top teams Penske and Ganassi: eight wins, ten fastest laps and thirteen poles, including at the Indy 500. And a 'third-should-have-been-first' in the 2009 IndyCar championship.

'IndyCar was a breath of fresh air,' Briscoe said. 'The politics in F1 were overwhelming.'

Top right: Ryan Briscoe was the first junior member in Toyota's Formula One team. Between 2002 and 2009 the ambitious, cashed-up Japanese manufacturer entered 140 grands prix without a win. By the time of their withdrawal Briscoe was long gone, released without ever having faced the starter's lights. A waste of exceptional talent and, for one of the world's most successful car companies, a rare and very public humiliation.

Bottom right: Ryan Briscoe (below, centre), flanked by Toyota's inaugural grand prix drivers Mika Salo (left) and Allan McNish (right), and at the feet of the Toyota team's president Ove Andersson, a man so revered in Formula One that they called him *Påven*—the Pope. Andersson hand-picked Briscoe as the next star, but when Påven lost his job in Toyota's round robin of executive appointments and dismissals, Briscoe was gone too.

JAMES COURTNEY

James Courtney was pulled unconscious from the wreck of his Jaguar F1 car by world champion Michael Schumacher. In private testing at Monza in July 2002, the left-hand rear suspension of his car had pulled loose at 306 km/h at the Ascari chicane. The collision was measured at 67g.

'I woke with my eyes bleeding and unable to move the right side of my body,' Courtney said. Schumacher, testing his Ferrari, had pulled up immediately and was directing recovery. 'I spent a full year with dreadful migraines,' Courtney recalled. He'd been in line for the Jaguar F1 race drive the following year, but the

Dancing with the cars. James Courtney tested with the Jaguar Formula One team but his potential was cut short in a development session in which a component failure turned him into little more than a crash test dummy. Jaguar was owned by Ford and, like Toyota, the auto giant was not adept at Formula One. Over five seasons they were winless across 85 races. Courtney carved out a stellar career in Australian Supercar racing—and appeared on television's *Dancing with the Stars* in 2007.

crash curtailed his assault on the 2002 British Formula Three championship and, without that title, the Formula One drive was less assured. He'd been leading the F3 championship comfortably, and bravely returned after the crash to salvage second in the title. But the F1 drive did not come.

Courtney was a karting phenomenon—the only Australian to win the Junior Karting World Championship, living in Brescia near the Tony Kart factory while still a teenager. His motorsport progression was spectacular. He won the British Formula Ford Championship and earned a place with the Jaguar Junior Team in Formula Three. He won his first F3 race, and that set the tone of his junior career.

In 2003, Courtney headed for Japan and won the Japanese Formula Three Championship, then entered their Super GT series. But as Neil Crompton, his friend and mentor, recalled in an interview with Courtney: 'I was sitting in a car with you [James] and you said—"I want to come home."' A decade on the road had been enough.

Courtney returned to Australia and won the 2010 Supercar Championship. He has been on the podium four times at the Bathurst 1000.

WILL POWER AND WILL DAVISON

Will Power and Will Davison tested Australian Paul Stoddart's Minardi at Misano, Italy, on 30 November 2004. After 22 laps each, Power had a best time of 1 minute 11.79 seconds. Davison did 1 minute 11.9 seconds. Nothing between them. Neither paid for the test. A combination of the Australian Grand Prix Corporation, Mark Webber—who'd driven for Minardi—and Stoddart's own generosity took care of that. 'I was particularly pleased to help them realise the dream of a lifetime by driving an F1 car,' Stoddart said. 'Let's hope at least one of them is able to follow in Mark Webber's footsteps.' But it didn't happen. Neither Will could find a way.

Speed had been a family tradition for both Wills. Davison's grandfather Lex had won the Australian Grand Prix four times, and his father Richard was Australian Formula Two champion. Power's grandfather William, for whom he was named, was a motorcycle champion and in 1915 set a Toowoomba-to-Brisbane speed record over the Great Dividing Range. Power's dad, Bob, raced against Richard Davison in Formula Two.

The two Wills had been circling each other in British F3: Davison was eighth in the 2003 championship, while Power, with fewer races contested, was fourteenth. In 2005, along with Ryan Briscoe, they drove some races in the A1 Grand Prix series for Australian Alan Docking's team, which was owned by Alan Jones. The series rewarded nations, not individuals, and the team that included Jones' son Christian came thirteenth.

Will Davison and Will Power were both primed to follow the Formula One talent who had driven for Minardi. Alumni include Fernando Alonso, Alex Zanardi and Mark Webber. Giancarlo Minardi started the team in 1985 and sold it to Paul Stoddart in 2001, who then sold it to Red Bull in 2005.

Power took his talent to America—funded in part by motor-racing and business entrepreneur Craig Gore (sentenced in Queensland in 2020 to five years' gaol for fraud). Power drove for Gore's ambitious Team Australia in Champ Car and in 2006 he claimed sixth outright and Rookie of the Year. He translated that into an IndyCar Series victory in 2014 and victory in the Indianapolis 500 in 2018, the only Australian ever to win the great race. At the beginning of the 2021 season, he was fifth on the all-time list of IndyCar winners, with 39 race wins, and with 62 poles he was second only behind Mario Andretti.

Will Davison returned to Australia, won the Bathurst 1000 twice and in 2021, after seventeen years in Supercars, joined championship-defending Dick Johnson Racing, knocking on the door of his first title. Paul Stoddart keeps one of his glorious V10 Minardis in Australia—converted to two seats so it can take VIPs for guest rides at the Australian F1 Grand Prix. Will Davison is one of its drivers.

SCOTT DIXON

Scott Dixon tested for Prost and toyed with Williams but remained true to IndyCar, where he has won six championship titles—only one behind all-time great A.J. Foyt. He has been with the one team, Chip Ganassi Racing, for nineteen years; with 50 race wins, the third-highest ever, his loyalty has paid off. He won the Indianapolis 500 for Ganassi in 2008, the only New Zealander to do so, three years after he declined further negotiations with Williams. Mark Webber was signed by Williams, most likely as a result.

'I couldn't believe the sheer pace of the F1 cars, how nimble they were,' Dixon said at his Indianapolis home. He dodged a bullet when he didn't go with Prost.

Indianapolis 500 winner and multiple IndyCar champion Scott Dixon tested twice with Williams Formula One in 2004—at Paul Ricard in dry conditions and two weeks later at Catalunya in the wet. Both times he was within range of the team's regular drivers Ralf Schumacher and Marc Gené. The tests were an audition: Juan Pablo Montoya was on the move to McLaren and Dixon was in the frame for a race seat in the Williams FW26 BMW.

The team, owned by four-time world champion Alain Prost, was already in financial difficulties when he tested. By 2002 it was bankrupt. When Williams came calling, he'd already won his first IndyCar series. 'Do you go to Formula One and be a test driver and lost forever, or do you continue racing?' Scott opined.

Dixon's long-term manager is Stefan Johansson, a Formula One veteran of some note—twelve podiums and 88 career points from 79 starts with teams including Ferrari and McLaren. 'I'm convinced Scott could have won one or more world titles in F1,' he said. Dixon simply doesn't know. 'Emma [his wife] asks me occasionally: Am I sad I didn't chase Formula One? My answer is: "I think we made the best choice, absolutely."'

Dixon was born in Australia but travels on a New Zealand passport and talks like a Kiwi, despite his time in the States. New Zealand has honoured him as both a Member and Companion of its Order of Merit. Only a knighthood remains.

KEN KAVANAGH AND KEITH CAMPBELL

Ken Kavanagh and Keith Campbell were Australian legends in European motorcycle racing. At Ulster in 1952 on a Norton 350, Kavanagh became the first Australian to win a world championship motorcycle grand prix. Campbell went one better. In 1957, as a works rider for Moto Guzzi, he won the 350cc World Championship, the first Australian to claim a motorcycle world title. They were stars in Italy. Kavanagh had been a works rider for Moto Guzzi too and his celebrity status was reinforced when he courted the vivacious Countess Isabella Siotto Pintor of Bergamo.

In 1958, Maserati offered them each a 250F Formula One car. They both accepted. Kavanagh tested in December 1957 on the Autodromo di Modena and was excited by his transition to four wheels. The relationship with Maserati started with high hopes.

In the mix and match of mechanical and body parts, it's likely that Kavanagh's car was the one Fangio used to win the 1957 world championship. Campbell may have secured Stirling Moss's Monaco GP winner.

Campbell was committed to Norton as a works rider in 1958, but Kavanagh flew with the Formula One teams to Argentina for the first round of the world championship. When battle-scarred Frenchman Jean Behra (he'd torn off his ear in a race crash), a favourite son of Maserati, arrived without a car, Kavanagh gave his up. Behra drove it to fifth.

But there wouldn't be more world championships. Kavanagh's entry in the Monaco Grand Prix was refused by organisers because of his novice status, and although he qualified for the Belgian Grand Prix, his engine broke on the last lap of practice and he was a non-starter. Instead, both riders raced in non-championship

Ken Kavanagh (Maserati 250F, leading) claimed eighteenth in the non-championship BRDC International Trophy at Silverstone in May 1958. The race was a Down Under affair. Jack Brabham was fifth, Bruce McLaren ninth; New Zealanders Ronnie Moore (here chasing Kavanagh two places behind) and Ray Thackwell both retired. And Count Stephen Ouvaroff, a Russian-born Australian who won the 1955 Queensland Grand Prix, was twentieth. Ouvaroff competed in the minor classes without F1 ambitions.

events—Campbell was ninth in the Glover Trophy at Goodwood in April 1958, won by Mike Hawthorn, with Jack Brabham second. Tragically, it would be his last drive.

On 13 July 1958, 27-year-old Campbell crashed in the 500cc Grand Prix de Cadours, near Toulouse, and was killed.

In March 1959, Kavanagh entered the next Glover Trophy. On lap ten, he spun backwards into the pit entrance and spectators were injured. That, too, was his last race. He returned to motorcycle racing, retired in 1960 and passed away at his home in Bergamo in 2019, aged 95.

16

AND THEN THE STARS CAME OUT
Craig Lowndes
Wayne Gardner
Mick Doohan
Mark Skaife

WHEN YOU'RE A MOTORSPORT CHAMPION IN ANY DISCIPLINE, Formula One opportunities just occasionally fall in your lap. They're guest rides, not meant to be serious, but there's no driver (or rider) yet who hasn't grasped the chance to prove their mettle. It's in their DNA. Four Australians, two of them motorcycle world champions, have seized the moment.

CRAIG LOWNDES

Seven-time Bathurst 1000 winner and three-time Supercars champion Craig Lowndes is the only Australian to lap the fabled Mount Panorama at an average speed greater than 200 km/h. It was 2011, and Lowndes had just three laps in the

Skyline at Mount Panorama, recognisable worldwide as one of motor racing's greatest challenges. In 2011, Craig Lowndes crested it at better than 250 km/h in the McLaren MP4-23 aero-car, so fast down Conrod Straight that the helicopter could not keep up. There have been moves to bring a top open-wheel formula to the Bathurst circuit. It will never pass Formula One safety standards but in 2021 the new Australian Gold Star formula, S5000, was confirmed for Mount Panorama competition.

McLaren MP4-23, the later-banned ground-effects F1 car that had carried Lewis Hamilton to his first world championship back in 2008. (The car was so well equipped with aerodynamic aids that it had triggered a new set of F1 regulations in order to level the field.) Supercars rely mainly on mechanical grip for their traction. Aerodynamic grip, at F1 level, was a world away from Lowndes' direct experience. His brief encounter at Mount Panorama was all the more impressive because of his lack of seat time.

Lowndes lapped Mount Panorama in 1 minute 50.088 seconds (203.17 km/h), just 0.678 seconds behind 2009 F1 world champion Jenson Button. Lowndes' one and only F1 drive was the result of a promotion mounted by his and Button's mutual telco sponsor. Button was equally keen to drive Lowndes' Supercar.

'Jenson was excited just to be at the Mountain,' Lowndes said. 'I spent an hour driving him around in a road car, explaining the track to him.'

Button was astounded. 'Normally I can learn a track in one or two laps. This one has taken me half a day,' he exclaimed.

When Button went out on his installation lap in the F1 car, Lowndes went to a place at the bottom of the circuit where he could watch Button's braking points. They were learning from each other.

When it was over, Lowndes was elated. 'Look at the traces,' he smiled. (Traces are the moment-by-moment descriptions of speed and dynamics generated by onboard telemetry. Teams use them, among other things, to compare the skills of their drivers.)

'I was quicker than him in all the slow corners—6–8 km/h better mid-corner. He was much quicker in anything that was high speed,' a delighted Lowndes said. 'It was amazing.' Predictably, Button had been faster in places where aero-grip counted. Lowndes wasn't going to take a risk in that zone. But Lowndes, so used to the Mountain and its nuances, was faster on the slow corners where mechanical grip took the ascendancy.

For Lowndes it was a bittersweet experience. Fourteen years before that, he'd spent a season in Europe trying to crack F3000, the feeder series to F1. The opportunity had been set up by his team owner in Australia, the late Tom Walkinshaw, who also owned a British-based F1 team. Walkinshaw had placed Lowndes with independent team owner Helmut Marko; his teammate was the mega-wealthy and mega-talented Juan Pablo Montoya. In neither case did the odds favour him. He returned, without a Formula One drive, to carve out a stellar career in Australia. But his three F1 laps of Mount Panorama left everyone wondering what might have been.

WAYNE GARDNER

In 1987, Wayne Gardner became the first Australian to win the World 500cc Motorcycle Championship, forerunner to MotoGP. His victory was instrumental in securing a world championship round for Australia, and he won that inaugural title race at Phillip Island in 1989. The images of his race celebration are etched in motorsport history. Long before Mark Webber adopted the persona, Gardner invented 'Aussie grit'. But by 1992, with eighteen world title race wins, Gardner was ready to move on. He finished a fighting second in his last motorcycle grand prix in South Africa in September 1992 and showcased himself in a Lotus 107B Formula One car at the Australian F1 Grand Prix eight weeks later. It was a massive promotion for the Grand Prix: Gardner, in an open-face helmet—all the better to see him with—did three laps in Team Lotus's spare car. It was supposed to have been just that—a promotion—but it stirred something deeper in Gardner. His determined Adelaide performance impressed Team Lotus and earned him 25 laps with the team at a Snetterton development day in 1993. But Lotus, at the time in the hands of Australia's Peter Collins, was in its financial death throes and Gardner's test came to nothing.

Wayne Gardner harboured Formula One ambitions. The 1987 World 500cc Motorcycle Champion impressed with a guest drive of the Lotus 107B in a promotion for the 1992 Australian Grand Prix at Adelaide, here being counselled by the car's regular driver, Mika Häkkinen. When his Formula One hopes did not come to fruition, Gardner turned to touring cars. In 1995 he was part of a Bathurst 1000 1-2-3 by Australia's international stars: Larry Perkins, first; Alan Jones, second; Wayne Gardner, third.

MICK DOOHAN

When five-time motorcycle world champion Mick Doohan—the fourth-highest motorcycle championship achiever of all time—lapped Spain's 4.65-kilometre Catalunya grand prix circuit in Williams' FW19 Formula One car, he did it 5 seconds faster than he had on his own record-breaking Honda NSR500 grand prix bike. 'I had to convince myself to go faster through a corner than I'm used to,' he said, highlighting the dynamic difference between two wheels and four. It was 1998; Doohan was chasing the fifth of his consecutive world titles, and a tobacco industry sponsor had brought him together with F1 world champion Jacques Villeneuve and four-time World Rally Champion Tommi Mäkinen. It was a promotion made for media—three world-title holders in three disciplines— sampling each other's race machines . . . except Williams steadfastly refused to let their man Villeneuve throw a leg over Doohan's race Honda.

In hindsight, Williams could have done it better. Both Doohan and Mäkinen spun on their out laps: 'I have to learn to be more relaxed about the power,' Doohan grinned. Four laps later he was driving 'like I'm going to the shops to get newspapers and milk', but faster than he'd ever been on his bike—and more

Opposite: The three fastest men in the world in 1998: Jacques Villeneuve (left), Mick Doohan (centre) and Tommi Mäkinen (right). Five-time World 500cc Motorcycle Champion Doohan's only Formula One drive was at a PR day set up by their tobacco-company sponsor. Doohan is closer to four-wheel sport now than he was then. He has been chair of Karting Australia and of the Australian Motorsport Council, and he avidly follows his son Jack's international career as a Red Bull Junior.

Above: Mick Doohan's drive in the Williams FW19 was brief. The car, designed in the main by Adrian Newey with input from Geoff Willis and Patrick Head, had won the 1997 world constructors' and drivers' championships, but its drivers still described it as a difficult car—'like driving on ice'. As of 2021, the FW19 remains the last Williams chassis to win a world title.

safely, too, according to Williams. A reasonable percentage of the specialist media had turned up for the occasion and they went away with little more than a photo opportunity. A grand chance to see what Doohan and Mäkinen could really do in a Formula One car had never really eventuated.

MARK SKAIFE

Mark Skaife was fixated on pursuing a F3000 season in Europe in 1993 as a step up to Formula One. Skaife was born to be a Formula One driver. In 1992, he'd won his second Australian Gold Star championship, his first Australian touring car title and his second Bathurst 1000. Then he got a call-up to drive a Jordan F1 car as part of the prelude to the 1992 Australian Grand Prix in Adelaide. But it turned out to be at the Colonnades shopping centre, south of the city. He was kitted up, doing laps of the perimeter of the car park for the photographers.

Skaife is the most positive of people. The association with Eddie Jordan's team was 'no bad thing', but in the pay-to-play days of Formula One, he couldn't raise the backing for a European assault, so he remained in Australia. He won one more Gold Star championship at a time when natural ability was being supplemented by technology and data acquisition. He applied that technical discipline to closed-saloon racing and went on to claim five Australian touring car titles, win six Bathurst 1000s and achieve 90 supercars victories before retiring from active competition in 2011. Formula One's loss was Australia's gain. Skaife has become one of the most influential people in domestic motor racing, designing circuits, guiding development of regulations and taking a deep dive into the sport's administration.

Top right: In 2010 Mark Skaife (left) drove with Craig Lowndes (right) in just two races—the Bathurst 1000 and the Phillip Island 500—and they won both. It's an immense leap from Supercars to Formula One, and neither succeeded in their international ambitions. The reverse move is equally difficult. Larry Perkins indisputably made the switch with six Bathurst wins; of the European Formula One contingent, only Jacky Ickx won Bathurst—with Allan Moffat in 1977.

Bottom right: Back to the future: It was only 1992—not that long ago—but Mark Skaife's sole Formula One drive, in the Jordan 192, circumnavigating an Adelaide car park, had him rushing past spectators, kerbside, without protection. Even back then it was unthinkable.

17

THE DESIGNERS
Chris Dyer
Willem Toet
Malcolm Oastler
Sam Michael
Ralph Bellamy
John Joyce

'IN MY DAY THERE WAS AN AUSSIE OR A KIWI IN THE workshop or the pits at every Formula One team, bar Ferrari,' Steve Roby, engineer for McLaren in the 1970s, told me from his home in the USA. 'From New Zealand's Roy Billington, Jack Brabham's long-serving chief engineer, through to Australian Wayne Eckersley on Alan Jones' championship Williams and Alastair Caldwell with McLaren, they had an unsurpassed work ethic.' Over 70 years, Australasians have been the backbone of Formula One, as engineers and designers.

It's a long way from Bendigo, Victoria, to the Formula One podium, celebrating alongside seven-time world champion Michael Schumacher as his engineer. Chris Dyer grew up following 500cc motorcycle racing, a huge fan of Wayne Gardner. But he became Australia's most capped Formula One engineer of the post-Tauranac era, one of a small group of Down Under specialists who've helped drive the development of Formula One.

CHRIS DYER

Chris Dyer *did* work for Ferrari. He was Michael Schumacher's trusted race engineer when they won the 2003 and 2004 world titles, and he'd been his performance engineer, a much more intimate role, essentially a coaching position, for the two world titles before that. 'Michael was the best driver I'll ever work with,' Dyer, in his early fifties and now in a senior role with Renault's Alpine F1 team, said from the UK. 'He was also the nicest person you'd want to work with. I have enormous respect for him.'

Dyer is one of Australian motor racing's great achievers. Jack Brabham won three world championships. Dyer has three to his credit too—two with Schumacher and one with Kimi Räikkönen in 2007—all three at Ferrari. Bespectacled, Bendigo-born

In 2007, Chris Dyer engineered Kimi Räikkönen to the closest of world championship victories, one point clear of Lewis Hamilton and Fernando Alonso. Räikkönen had joined Ferrari at the start of the season and at the first race, the Australian Grand Prix, he claimed pole position, fastest lap and race victory. The remainder of the championship was a rollercoaster of victories (five) and opportunities lost in mechanical failures and strategy decisions. In 2021, Räikkönen's world championship remained Ferrari's most recent world title.

Dyer was Australia's man in red, perched on the Ferrari pod on pit lane. He worked with Schumacher, technical genius Ross Brawn and dynamo Jean Todt when they delivered Ferrari its best ever era—six consecutive world constructors' titles, five consecutive drivers' titles for Schumacher, and 72 grand prix victories. In the highly charged political atmosphere of Ferrari, it couldn't last.

Schumacher and Brawn both left at the end of 2006, Todt in 2009.

When the politicians moved in, Dyer was made chief race engineer, in charge of both cars. During a grand prix it's a tactical role, acting instantly to call a pit stop or demand more pace in reaction to another team's movements. It's the place the buck stops.

In 2010, the world championship would be decided at the last grand prix at Abu Dhabi. Fernando Alonso (Ferrari) led on points; Mark Webber and Sebastian Vettel (Red Bull) were second and third. It was match racing at the highest level. On lap 12, Webber brushed a wall and came to the pits for fresh tyres. Ferrari called Alonso in to cover him. But they'd covered the wrong Red Bull. Alonso and Webber became trapped in slower traffic, and Vettel, in clear air, sprinted ahead to win the race and his first world championship.

'I knew 30 seconds after Alonso drove out of the pit lane, we'd got it wrong,' Chris told me. 'It was just torture. As soon as the race was over, I went to look for somewhere to hide. I headed for [team principal] Stefano Domenicali's office. I knew he wouldn't be there. But when I stepped inside, there was [Ferrari chairman] Luca di Montezemolo with Piero Ferrari (Enzo's son). I'd thrown myself to the wolves.' He was gone two weeks later.

Dyer entered Formula One through Tom Walkinshaw Racing, the official Holden team in Australia, as a data engineer, and helped develop the VR Commodore with which Craig Lowndes won the 1996 Australian Touring Car Championship. In 1997, Lowndes took off to Europe to drive a season of F3000 and Dyer joined Walkinshaw's Arrows F1 team. He was made data engineer for world-champion Damon Hill.

Three years on, Dyer handed his CV to Ferrari's Ross Brawn. His first interview was in Ross's home; his second was in the Cavallino restaurant opposite the gates of the Ferrari factory. He joined Ferrari in 2001.

In the aftermath of Abu Dhabi, Dyer filled his time completing an MBA and working for BMW's motorsport division. In 2016 he joined Renault Sport (now Alpine) as head of vehicle performance. The Renault position is factory based, which suits a family man with two pre-teen children. In 2021, he was looking forward to welcoming a new driver to Alpine. Fernando Alonso was coming back to F1. Dyer expected the dynamics to be 'interesting'.

WILLEM TOET

Willem Toet was frustrated by Ferrari. The Dutch-born, Melbourne-raised aerodynamicist had been promised a wind tunnel when he joined the Scuderia in 1994. 'Montezemolo wanted it to be a statement so they hired Renzo Piano to design it. It took a year longer to build than it should have and it made a noise like an aeroplane,' Toet claimed from his Swiss base. 'All I wanted was a big box.' He found some satisfaction a decade later when Ferrari hired the much smaller wind tunnel at Sauber, where Toet was then working, 'because after the Schumacher years they'd made no progress on their own,' he claimed.

Within the tight-knit technical community of Formula One, Toet is a legend, some say of his own making—a master of the black art of aerodynamics, renowned for his unbending principles (he has 'fired' two Formula One teams because their standards did not align with his) and his total commitment to winning. Money is not the motivator: 'When Jean Todt hired me from Benetton to Ferrari, he asked: what did I want? I said, "The same as at Benetton." "You're not very good at this," he replied, and gave me a substantial raise.'

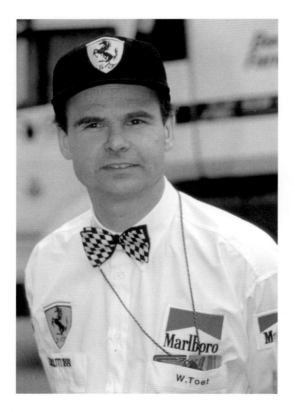

Willem Toet justifiably earned his reputation as an aerodynamic specialist in the era when Formula One cars began to rely more on downforce than mechanical grip, and lap speeds improved thanks to greater cornering ability. As Formula One seeks to become carbon neutral and more cost effective, hugely expensive wind tunnels—the mainstay of F1 supremacy for three decades, and Toet's speciality—are now coming under threat, possibly to be replaced entirely by sophisticated computational fluid dynamics.

In the nicest possible way, Toet is F1's nutty professor. 'I'm excitable, I know,' he said. With his Bachelor of Science majoring in biology from La Trobe University, he has spent more than twenty years in Formula One working out how to make cars go faster through the air (science) and how to make them more drivable (biology)—'why one jet fighter pilot can live and another die'.

Formula One was a giant leap from club motor racing, where he started in Melbourne.

Four Formula One teams have benefited from Toet's unique form of obsession: Benetton, Ferrari, BAR and Sauber. In retirement from active racing, he became a consultant to Sauber's customer department. It gives him access to their computational fluid dynamics. His latest project helped Kenyan long-distance runner Eliud Kipchoge become the first runner to break the marathon's two-hour barrier.

MALCOLM OASTLER

Malcolm Oastler worked with Willem Toet on the highly ambitious BAR F1 car, in the tobacco company–funded race team built around world champion Jacques Villeneuve. Oastler was technical director; Toet joined BAR's aero department after he was released from Ferrari. 'We had to have him,' Oastler said, 'even if he did turn up at race meetings with flashing LED lights in his bow tie.'

Oastler was a serious junior racer. He was second in the 1983 Australian Formula Ford Driver to Europe Series, but 'ran out of money and will'. In 1984, he took off on a bicycle tour of Europe and found work with an Australian team based in the UK, racing Formula Fords. Oastler traded his engineering skills for occasional drives.

In 1985 he answered a help-wanted ad in *Autosport* for a design draftsman at Reynard Motorsport. Former racer Adrian Reynard was one of the sport's most prolific constructors and under his guidance, Oastler became a multitalented professional. He stayed with the team for seventeen years, a lifetime in motor racing, right up to the end when the company filed for bankruptcy in 2002, a result of runaway ambition. 'There were 30 people at Reynard when I started and 300 when it finished,' Oastler recalled.

Oastler designed the 1995 Reynard 951, which won the Indy 500 in the hands of Jacques Villeneuve, sponsored by British American Tobacco. Four years later, Villeneuve's manager Craig Pollock built an F1 team around his driver. BAR-Reynard was revealed in 1999.

'The car wasn't easy to drive,' Oastler said. And the team wasn't easy to manage. Acrimony set in—Pollock and Reynard fought so badly that BAR got

Malcolm Oastler earned a first-class honours degree in mechanical engineering and applied it to building some of the fastest cars in the world. His contemporaries say his work on the chassis for the 340 km/h Indianapolis speed bowl (where his Reynard won in 1995) honed his skills for Formula One. He was instrumental in the design of the BAR Formula One program, which morphed into Honda Racing, became Brawn Formula One in 2009, and evolved into the dominating Mercedes team.

rid of them both. Reynard was replaced as chassis supplier and then declared bankruptcy. Oastler, simply, was collateral damage.

'I was keen to showcase myself. I'd just been sacked,' Oastler said. But he joined Ford-owned Jaguar F1, another team in turmoil. Instead of the freewheeling Reynard, he was now working for a corporation, filling in engineering reports and drowning in a sea of paperwork.

Oastler retreated to Australia. On his farm in Bega he builds unusual vehicles—a Jaguar-powered open-wheeler in the style of a prewar Auto Union; a V8-engine motorcycle; and a hill-climb car weighing 300 kilograms and developing 400 horsepower, 'a moon rocket'. He used it to win the Australian Hill Climb Championship, a title he has claimed five times.

SAM MICHAEL

Sam Michael knows what it's like to have a Formula One team go bankrupt under him. In 1993, aged just 22, he'd secured his first position in F1, with Lotus, living his data-engineering dream in the back of the F1 pit. A year later: 'I had an inkling something was wrong. I rang an engineer at the plant and he said, "No, all good here." But when I turned up at the factory it was empty. Everyone was gone. A security guard wouldn't even let me in to pick up my stuff.' Michael called Greg 'Peewee' Siddle. Within a week he'd been placed at Jordan, en route to a career that encompassed Williams and McLaren at near the highest level. The 'Peewee push' could never be underestimated.

In 1991, Michael was completing a degree in the new science of data acquisition when he joined Siddle and Australian Formula Ford champion Mark Larkham in their assault on the Australian Drivers' Championship.

They let the boy-genius drive the truck to Adelaide for the 1991 Australian F1 Grand Prix: 'I was blown away,' Michael smiled. 'I was obsessed with the sound of the V12s and V10s. You could feel it. I rang my parents from a phone box and said: "This is for me."' Peewee introduced Sam to Peter Wright from Lotus, and he showed Wright his thesis. 'You've got a job if you come to England,' Wright told him and met him at the train station when he arrived.

Later, at Jordan, Michael helped build the team's first seven-post rig, a full-size device that can be programmed to simulate the loads and forces of any racetrack. It's an engineer's dream: to be able to test in the laboratory to achieve repeatable and understandable results. 'It's exactly the opposite of the public face of Formula One, which has to look unpredictable to sell tickets,' Michael said.

They were pioneering days: 'We couldn't cheat but we could take the rules to the nth degree—the test being "Could I stand in front of the regulator and defend it?"' At Williams, Michael was promoted to technical director. 'Frank, we've been protested,' he said to his team owner. 'That's fantastic news,' Frank Williams replied. 'No one protests shit cars.'

Michael lived through an age of accelerated technical change—seamless-shift gear boxes, double diffusers, fan-assisted brakes, driver-activated F-ducts. Many were ultimately banned, but all were worth trying on: 'A 0.2-second improvement in lap time could cost $500,000.'

He worked closely with the greats of the sport, like Frank Williams, 'who willingly sold his £22 million [A$40 million] Falcon jet to fund workshop

Hitting the mark. Daniel Ricciardo places his McLaren MCL35M directly on the stop point so 16 mechanics, like bees in a bottle, can execute a 2-second pit stop (the technique is Sam Michael's legacy to the team).

In 2021, one of Sam Michael's greatest achievements in Formula One was under threat. Michael is an expert in data acquisition and, importantly, in its application to improve efficiency. At McLaren, working with principal Ron Dennis (right), he halved pit-stop times by transforming mechanics' actions into subconscious reactions. In 2021, the FIA introduced new regulations dictating that mechanics' reaction times could not be faster than those considered possible for a human being.

improvements'—even though it meant that the incapacitated Williams would be severely curtailed. 'Frank had an apartment in the factory so he could work around the clock.'

Then there was Ron Dennis at McLaren. 'Every mechanic on the floor looked up to him because he used to be one of them. He was obsessed with preventative maintenance. He'd take a good car and strip it. It seemed crazy; in many cases he'd find nothing. But you had to respect him because of his wins.'

Michael applied the lessons. 'When I joined McLaren, they were doing pit stops in 4 seconds.' He changed not only the technique but the psychology of each of the 24 people involved in the stop—'how to make actions come from the subconscious'—and achieved the sport's first sub–2-second stops.

Now in Sydney, in harbourside Cremorne, he runs a software engineering consultancy that helps companies improve efficiency. He contributes to racing as a board member of the Australian Institute for Motor Sport Safety. Safety is his calling: 'I won nineteen grands prix with three teams, and in my whole career I never had a driver fatality.'

RALPH BELLAMY

Ralph Bellamy, from Sydney's Eastwood, helped design the Lotus 78, the world's first ground-effects car, in 1977. It changed the face of Formula One forever. 'It was a quantum leap,' Bellamy said. 'Once you've done it, you can't un-invent it.

Ralph Bellamy (left) became the next designer of Brabham racing cars after Ron Tauranac, working for Bernie Ecclestone (right), the new owner of Motor Racing Developments. Tauranac and Ecclestone had lasted just a year together before a clash of wills caused a permanent split. Bellamy, who'd enjoyed a long-term association with Tauranac, redesigned the Brabham BT34 'lobster claw' car into the BT37. The car had eighteen Formula One starts, but without success.

After that, every team had to have it.' Bellamy was a skilled designer, less so a media operator. He gave an interview to Peter Windsor, published in *Autocar*, revealing details and his involvement in the design. 'I heard Colin Chapman went ape,' he said. 'He never said a word to me, but he promoted me sideways into the passenger car division. I spent a year there while they raced my world-beating car.'

Bellamy had originally gone to Europe to go yacht racing. Instead, he joined Ron Tauranac as a draftsman at Brabham. In 25 years he worked across six Formula One teams. He arrived at the time Formula One cars were growing wings: 'I was never trained in aerodynamics but I had to start to pick up this new technology,' he said. That led to the Lotus 78. Despite Chapman's punishment, he rated Lotus as the best place he'd worked. 'You've got to have the money to do a good job and Team Lotus had the money and the infrastructure so that's where I did my best work.'

Bellamy returned to Australia the year Sam Michael arrived in Europe. 'For me, the 1970s were great years for Formula One racing,' he recalled. 'There were no pit stops. The whole field came around in one big snarling bunch. It was great racing . . . the competition was fantastic.'

JOHN JOYCE

John Joyce from Toowoomba was, in 1963, the first Australian designer to join Lotus. He had built a Formula Junior racing car and called it the Bowin Koala. (Bowin is an abbreviation of 'Born to Win'.) The Koala impressed Lotus and they invited him to England as a project engineer, soon to become chief development engineer. The 24-year-old Joyce was off like a shot.

He worked on, but was never credited for, the Lotus 49—the Formula One car built to take the Cosworth DFV motor—which was to have been Jim Clark's ticket to victory in the 1968 world championship before his death early in the season. Graham Hill took it to championship glory instead.

Joyce was given broad responsibility at Lotus—across formula racing, Indianapolis oval competition, and the company's road-car program. He had total responsibility for the Lotus 41 Formula Two car, and Colin Chapman, unusually, credited him with his development of the revolutionary Europa sports car. Lotus was simultaneously stimulating and stifling. Joyce was at odds with Chapman's 'lightweight at all costs' philosophy. The issue of safety weighed heavily.

In 1968, aged 30, he returned to Australia and rekindled Bowin Designs in the Sydney beachside suburb of Brookvale. His lightweight open-wheelers, built on Lotus principles, with a leaning towards strategic strengthening, dominated the

A modest, self-effacing person, John Joyce was justifiably proud of creating an entire brand of racing cars, pictured here (right) at an exclusively Bowin day at Sydney's Oran Park. Joyce built his Bowins into a Formula Ford force. They won four Driver to Europe Series championships in the 1970s and created the platform for John Leffler to become Australian champion. Joyce's ambitious export program in the UK and USA never truly worked.

Australian Formula Ford Championship in the 1970s. But Joyce had overestimated the capacity of the domestic market to support two local manufacturers (Garrie Cooper's Elfin was already established in South Australia). He built just 56 Bowins before resorting to general engineering. He is credited with designing the world's first automated deep fryer for commercial kitchens. He died in 2002.

18

SUPREME AUTHORITY
Michael Masi
Garry Connelly
Dr Michael Henderson

THE FORMULA ONE WORLD CHAMPIONSHIP WAS BORN in France and made global by Englishman Bernie Ecclestone. In 2021, it was owned by American venture capital company Liberty Media, contested by drivers from fourteen countries, scheduled to race in the grands prix of 22 nations. Formula One turns over US$2 billion [A$2.5 billion] a year and has a market capitalisation of US$5.6 billion [A$7.2 billion].

But when the drivers strap into their six-point racing harness, an invention of Australian Dr Michael Henderson, the field is effectively in the control of two other Australians, one of whom works for free. Garry Connelly is a chairman of F1 stewards and Michael Masi is FIA's F1 race director.

MICHAEL MASI

In the instant Romain Grosjean impacted at 192 km/h with the metal crash barrier in the 2020 Bahrain Grand Prix and his car became a fireball, Michael

---

On 29 November 2020, Romain Grosjean survived this fiery, high-speed impact at the Bahrain Grand Prix. His extrication from the blaze was a result of decades of incremental improvements in safety technology—and perhaps a great deal of good fortune. Formula One has strong memories of the fireballs of the '70s that claimed the lives of Piers Courage (1970) and Roger Williamson (1973), both at Zandvoort, and of Niki Lauda's escape from death at the Nürburgring in 1976.

Michael Masi (right, white shirt) directed the recovery of the shell of Romain Grosjean's Haas Ferrari VF-20 at the 2020 Bahrain Grand Prix, and the rebuilding of the safety fencing; within 90 minutes the race was back in action. On the restart lap, Lance Stroll's Racing Point BWT Mercedes rolled without injury to the driver, highlighting safety improvements.

Masi pressed the race's main abort button and triggered an emergency response. The explosion was like nothing F1 had experienced in 40 years. There was a time when the immolation of drivers was almost the norm—no less shocking, but expected. Masi had not even been born then. Nothing in his direct experience had prepared him for this moment. Yet in the next 27 seconds, while Grosjean fought for his life, Masi worked with calm precision to deploy resources, ignoring the cacophony around him. And when the immediate danger had passed, he directed the fast-paced recovery project that had the race restarted in 90 minutes.

Masi, 42, from Fairfield in Sydney's Western Suburbs, is Formula One's first career race director. He replaced Charlie Whiting, who for 20 years was the operational face of Formula One.

'I never wanted to be a race driver, but I always wanted to be in racing,' he said. He was a precocious, pedantic talent. When he went to the 1992 Adelaide F1 Grand Prix as a thirteen-year-old, in the days before the big screen, he took along his own portable TV so he could watch the action at the back of the circuit. He was a serial pest at the Sydney race team headquarters of Peewee Siddle in Granville and Supercar driver Mark Larkham at Wetherill Park. On the phone, he negotiated with category representative Procar to enter a Ferrari F355 Challenge in their sports car series. 'They never asked my age.' He was fifteen. They offered him a job. Four years later, the teenager managed his uncle Rudolf's Piccola Scuderia F3 team, and his driver, Peter Hackett, became the first Australian champion of the new F3 series. Then he got serious.

Garry Connelly enrolled him in a stewards' program, presenting a career path. In quick succession he worked in operations at Supercars, joined Motorsport Australia as project manager, and helped Singapore and South Korea start their grands prix. In South Korea he met then–F1 race director Charlie Whiting, who asked him about his future. 'I'd like to succeed you when the time comes,' Masi replied.

Back home, he was CEO of the world championship Rally Australia, 'my first CEO role', and then secretary of the Supercars Commission, sitting alongside director Tim Schenken in race control at the domestic touring-car races. Whiting was watching. In 2018, he invited Masi to help at eight F1 races, flying him around the world. The next year he was to be made race director of F3 and F2 to see if he could handle the giant leap to F1 sometime in the future.

But on 14 March 2019, Charlie Whiting was found dead in his hotel room in Melbourne. He had suffered a pulmonary embolism at 66. It was three days before the opening round of the world championship, just one day before the first practice session. Michael was asked by FIA president Jean Todt to step up.

Formula One race control is like a Hollywood representation of NASA Headquarters. It is approached via a long, airlocked corridor past security guards, and the level of accreditation rises exponentially. A complete wall of monitors, five deep and ten wide, faces tiered seats for upwards of twenty specialist operators. It's bathed in half-light and is hushed; communication is via headsets. Voices are seldom raised.

Charlie Whiting, who grew up in motor racing (he was a mechanic on the Bernie Ecclestone–owned Brabham that won Nelson Piquet two world championships) built race control from his own experience. Charlie multi-tasked. As well as race directing from central control, he insisted on starting each race, the domestic ones on the program as well, from the gantry high above the main straight.

In the shadow of Charlie. Michael Masi took to the stage at the 2019 Autosport Awards to accept the John Bolster Award on behalf of Charlie Whiting. The Bolster Award is given to a person or organisation that has made an exceptional contribution to motorsport technology. Commentator and former Formula One racer Martin Brundle said that Whiting 'was absolutely unique in our industry, business and sport'.

'I'm not trying to do everything Charlie did,' Michael said. 'We've appointed a permanent starter now and I stay in race control.' But, like Charlie, Michael is the FIA's safety delegate at each grand prix. Ensuring safety is a responsibility he shares with Garry Connelly.

GARRY CONNELLY

'We've had death threats. It affects me as it would any human being.' Garry Connelly's role in Formula One invites criticism from the fans, and more than occasionally creates frustration among the teams—at least until they settle down and re-read the rule book. Garry sits in judgement on the actions of the drivers, teams and sporting stakeholders in the world championship. He is one of just four chairmen of F1's stewards. It's an honorary position, a world away from his financial services business in the lee of Brisbane's Gabba cricket ground, nice art on the walls, inviting your trust. By his estimate, he's there maybe forty per cent of his time. The rest of his working life is spent trying to apply that same sense of balance in Formula One.

'The constitution of the FIA vests its stewards with supreme authority,' he said, and there's a certain air of steely self-belief in his voice. This is a man who

A chairman of the Formula One stewards, Brisbane's Garry Connelly has been a motorsport administrator for more than 40 years. His first official appointment was as NSW secretary of the Confederation of Australian Motor Sport. His organisational talent was recognised by senior officials of the inaugural F1 Australian Grand Prix in 1985, who invited him to promote a round of the World Rally Championship to a similar standard. Connelly's Rally Australia was three times voted international Rally of the Year.

has been intimidated by the best of them and not backed down. 'We are not there as mediators but as decision makers.'

Some of those decisions have been highly controversial and applied in dramatic circumstances. In 2017, Connelly came under personal fire when his stewards' team (three are at each GP) at the US Grand Prix acted instantly on a last-lap lunge by Max Verstappen on Kimi Räikkönen. Momentarily, Verstappen had put four wheels off the track—a no-no—and the stewards pounced with a 5-second penalty, without taking time for review. Max was in the driver's cool-down room, on global TV, waiting to be called to the podium when he got the news. It didn't endear Connelly to the twenty-year-old Dutchman. Death threats followed—not from Verstappen, but from outraged fans.

Garry Connelly (left) devised a stewarding system for Formula One, incorporating a panel of experienced rule makers and one racing driver to bring practical perspective to each incident. Australian world champion Alan Jones (right) worked with the FIA as a steward for many years. Connelly insisted that drivers' opinions should always be interpreted within the framework of the Formula One regulations.

'Our job is to make sure the podium represents a clear result,' Connelly said. 'But I explained to him: Kimi was entitled to his place and it had been taken from him wrongly.'

There are two books of rules for Formula One—sporting and technical—and each contains upwards of 1000 articles. 'The teams have people whose entire job it is to read and interpret them,' Connelly said. He doesn't know all the rules by heart, but he does know the one that pinged Verstappen, because he wrote it.

In 2010, the new president of the FIA, Jean Todt, asked Connelly to revise the sporting code, which 'hadn't been touched since 1954'. He set out to make the rules fairer and easier to understand. He eliminated the drive-through penalty as 'too harsh' and replaced it with the time-punishment that took out Verstappen.

Connelly had known Todt since they both rallied. Garry's wife Monique had organised for a tractor to pull Jean's rally car from a bog during the Rally of New Caledonia. It takes a special dedication to rise through the ranks of the FIA. In the late 1980s Connelly instigated Rally Australia, the world rally championship event, and won international acclaim for his innovations. That put him on many FIA committees.

'In a normal year I'm on probably fifteen long-haul flights,' he said. It's a privileged position, a look inside the sport that enthusiasts would kill for, but it's lonely too: 'I can't eat with the teams, can't get too close.' There's a hangover from stewards past: 'There were incidents of bias.' And he has to remain independent of Formula One too because he has to hold them to account. 'It's a matter of principle,' he said.

DR MICHAEL HENDERSON

'I'd not met Jochen Rindt before, but I dined with him at the 1970 Monza Grand Prix and I did my best to advocate the use of the six-point safety harness.' Dr Michael Henderson, sitting on his balcony overlooking Sydney's sparkling Pittwater, was recalling his moment of greatest frustration. Henderson, who went on to become executive director of traffic safety in New South Wales, director of the Traffic Accident Research Unit, and establish Crashlab, with the first test sled in Australia, is the inventor of the six-point harness for racing cars. In 2021, he was made an officer of the Order of Australia (AO) for his contribution to safety on and off the racetrack.

Henderson's six-point harness was a development of similar technology used by parachutists. 'Rindt was irrationally concerned about his crown jewels. I told him that crotch straps, fitted as a pair, are designed to bear on the pubic bones and not on the genital organs. They curl around each hip like a parachute harness.

Rindt would have none of it.' He crashed in that grand prix, submarined forward in his four-point harness, and suffered catastrophic fatal injuries. Henderson's six-point harnesses were made mandatory two years after Rindt's death.

Dr Henderson was an early director of the FIA Institute for Motor Sport Safety and Sustainability. In 1968 he wrote a book, *Motor Racing in Safety: The Human Factors*, and it became a guide to initiatives now regarded as the most basic requirements. In 1968, roll-over protection had not been mandated and helmets were rudimentary. Henderson mused: 'Will the day ever come when every driver is harnessed into his car, just as every pilot is harnessed into his aircraft?' His depressing conclusion was: 'I doubt it.' Happily, he was wrong.

Garry Connelly went on to become deputy chairman of the FIA Institute. It was on his watch—but by no means, he is quick to point out, was it his invention—that the 'halo' was introduced, the wishbone-shaped roll cage above the driver. The halo, according to Michael Masi, and confirmed by computer modelling, saved Romain Grosjean's life as his car carved through multiple layers of steel fencing.

Opposite: Jochen Rindt's Lotus 72 is removed from Monza's Parabolica curve at the 1970 Italian Grand Prix. The rear of the car, minus its aerodynamic wing, was hardly damaged and the front seems remarkably intact. Yet Rindt, who became Formula One's only posthumous world champion, died when crash impact forces caused him to submarine forward into the cockpit unrestrained by a six-point harness that might have saved him.

Above: Dr Michael Henderson straps himself into the Sigma Safety car, revealed at the 1968 Geneva Motor Show. Henderson and a group of safety experts, including Sergio Pininfarina and Ferrari's Mauro Forghieri, built the Sigma (for safety) to showcase concepts including built-in fire protection, a six-point body restraint system, and a driver safety cell with collapsible structures and head restraint. Henderson's work is still regarded as pivotal in the advancement of Formula One safety.

19

PUNCHING ABOVE OUR WEIGHT
In Search of the Next Champion

TYRE MAGNATE BOB JANE AND ADELAIDE TRAVEL AGENT
Bill O'Gorman were independently responsible for Australia securing a round of the Formula One world championship. Jane, four-time Australian Touring Car champion, ran the Australian Grand Prix for five years from 1980 to 1984 at his Calder Park racetrack on Melbourne's outskirts. It brought some of the cream of the F1 grid back to Australia, reigniting international interest twenty years after the Tasman Series had ceased. But, with the exception of Alan Jones' Williams FW07 in 1980, the small field was almost exclusively driving small-bore, 1.6-litre, Ford-engined RALTs, not Formula One cars. Enthusiasm for the concept was running out concurrently with Jane's contract. In South Australia, Bill O'Gorman, a true enthusiast, was seized with an idea: why not run a world championship to celebrate the 150th anniversary of the state? So he wrote a letter to the premier.

The two giants of the F1 Australian Grand Prix. They called Ron Walker 'Big Red'. Bernard Charles Ecclestone was simply 'Bernie'. The pair shared an incredible rapport. The Melbourne businessman, who died in 2018, became one of Bernie's most trusted confidantes. Enthusiasts still argue that Melbourne 'stole' the grand prix from Adelaide. In truth it was unlikely to have survived without Walker's intervention and his dedicated support.

In 1983, South Australia's premier John Bannon asked Vern Schuppan, winner of the Le Mans 24 Hour, to call Bernie Ecclestone and press the case for Adelaide hosting a world F1 championship grand prix. Ecclestone, known universally by just one name—Bernie—had not been a fan of the idea.

'You don't get it. No one is interested in going to Australia. No one's heard of Adelaide,' Bernie, the head of the Formula One Constructors' Association, told Schuppan. 'I responded that the street circuit had support from the city council and the state government, and that it had a budget. He should be looking at this seriously,' Schuppan said.

To reinforce his point, Schuppan jumped in an Elfin F5000 car and drove at speed around Adelaide's East Terrace, closed specially for the occasion. Simultaneously, CAMS—now Motorsport Australia—employed Tim Schenken, just retired from active racing, to reinforce its F1 credibility.

In late 1983, Vern Schuppan drove his Elfin F5000 around Adelaide's East Terrace with a video camera mounted on the front suspension. The Adelaide police had closed the road, but had not told the surprised lawn-waterer. Schuppan's video was used to convince Bernie Ecclestone that an Australian grand prix was feasible.

'Fair Dinkum Formula One'—the Formula One world had to learn a new language. The Adelaide race, at the end of each season, embraced the city almost as much as the grand prix in Monaco. It rewrote the manual on building a street circuit and made Formula One an intrinsic part of its CBD. The collapse of the State Bank of South Australia in 1991 and the restructuring of state finances made it difficult for Adelaide to sustain the grand prix under pressure from Formula One to increase its investment.

It was a bid of Olympian proportions, extraordinary in its intricacy. A solution was found for every roadblock, and in London, following the 1984 British Grand Prix, John Bannon agreed terms with Bernie. Adelaide would have the rights to hold a grand prix, initially, for three years, for US$2 million [A$2.6 million] a year. The beautiful road circuit through the Adelaide Park Lands touched the CBD as well, so the grand prix truly incorporated the city. The 1985 Australian Grand Prix was promoted as 'Fair Dinkum F1' and was the fiftieth Australian Grand Prix, war years excluded, since Phillip Island in 1928.

At 10 a.m. on Friday 1 November 1985, Alan Jones, world champion in 1980 and the only Australian in the field, was given the singular honour of opening the first practice session with one lap, solo, in his Haas Lola. Eleven years later, Melbourne stole the race.

'I remember the day well,' former South Australian premier Dean Brown told the ABC. The Liberal leader had just won the state election. 'The day after I'd been sworn in, I received a telephone call from Ron Walker, who revealed a contract had been signed in extreme secrecy with Bernie almost a year before.' Walker, the former Melbourne lord mayor, and Victorian premier Jeff Kennett had kickstarted the Victorian Major Events Company to attract world-leading sports

On 3 November 1985, Nigel Mansell (Williams Honda) led the first F1 Australian Grand Prix into the first corner but retired with transmission failure on lap one. Mansell's teammate Keke Rosberg won the 82-lap, 309-kilometre grand prix in 35-degree heat. Only eight cars finished. Alan Jones, driving in his 100th grand prix, retired the troublesome Haas Lola THL-1 Hart on lap 21 after driving from the rear of the grid to sixth.

The first lap of the first Australian Grand Prix at Albert Park, 10 March 1996. Martin Brundle (Jordan Peugeot) launched off the back of David Coulthard (McLaren Mercedes) and Johnny Herbert (Sauber Ford) and barrel-rolled, stopping the race. Incredibly, Brundle got back to the pits, ran up pit lane and claimed the team's spare car for the restart, only to have another collision and retire on lap one. Damon Hill (Williams Renault) won the grand prix and went on to win the world championship.

to Victoria. They'd spotted a weakness in the F1 association with Adelaide. Bernie, by then chief of FOM (Formula One Management), had become frustrated with his dealings with South Australian authorities. 'It took 10 minutes to sign the deal [with Melbourne],' Bernie told media. The last Australian F1 Grand Prix in Adelaide was held in November 1995. The first in Melbourne was in March 1996.

In 2019, the Victorian government agreed with F1's owners, Liberty Media, to exercise its two-year option to lock in the Australian F1 Grand Prix through to 2025. In a statement announcing its contractual roll-over, the Department of Premier and Cabinet pointed to an economic benefit of $1.8 billion derived annually from Melbourne's four major events—the AFL Grand Final, the Australian Open tennis tournament, the Spring Racing Carnival and the Australian Grand Prix. 'The Grand Prix takes Melbourne to the world,' the Department's media release said, 'with images beamed to an estimated global audience of 80 million, including in the key markets of China, India and Japan.'

Increasingly, the line between sport and business has blurred. It is near impossible today to equate the dreams of a young fan of making it in Formula One with the reality of the mountain that has to be climbed. Since 1950, 32 countries have held grands prix. Eleven of those have come on board since Australia signed up and only two have been from the European continent. The twenty drivers on the 2021 grid came from 14 nations, and the catchment for future world champions has become totally global.

In September 2019, Michael Smith, director of motorsport at Motorsport Australia, took a phone call from Laurent Mekies, sporting director of Scuderia Ferrari. He needed Michael's help. The FIA is a relatively small village. They all know each other, and the good guys tend to gravitate to one another.

Mekies knew Motorsport Australia and its capabilities. 'Australia fights well above its weight,' Smith said, without false modesty. It's true. The Australian F1 Grand Prix's initiatives were revolutionary on introduction, and are now the backbone of the efficient conduct of the world championship. Australia introduced the minute-by-minute guide, which now runs most grands prix and is at the forefront of training of volunteer officials. Australia's attention to detail has made grands prix more streamlined and safer.

Other nations have turned to Australia to coach them on how to do it. Motorsport Australia provided support teams of several hundred people to assist with the inauguration of the Singapore and Korean grands prix. Mentoring has turned into a business. When Russia signed up for F1, Motorsport Australia bid against other organisers for their start-up contract and won.

Laurent Mekies contracted Motorsport Australia to join Scuderia Ferrari to become the Asia-Pacific representative of its Ferrari Driver Academy. A private contractor in Mexico would handle the Americas, and Ferrari would take care of itself in Europe. Each year a total of ten young hopefuls aged between fourteen and eighteen would travel to Maranello in the hope that one or two might be selected to become part of Ferrari's internal training program. Asia-Pacific would contribute two of those candidates.

Laurent Mekies (left), sporting director of Scuderia Ferrari, with Formula One race director Michael Masi. Mekies' respect for Australian organisational ability led to the Ferrari Driver Academy appointing Motorsport Australia as its Asia-Pacific/Oceania representative.

It's more than likely the next F1 title contender is going to emerge from the academies. Red Bull Racing is the acknowledged pioneer. Four-time world champion Sebastian Vettel graduated cum laude from the Red Bull Junior program. Daniel Ricciardo is an alumnus. In 2021, red-hot nineteen-year-old New Zealander Liam Lawson was in the Red Bull program and eighteen-year-old Jack Doohan, son of five-time world MotoGP winner Mick, was an associate.

Ferrari grew its own F1 team leader, Charles Leclerc, and in 2021 proudly sent Mick Schumacher, son of its all-time legend Michael, up to Formula One—not in a Ferrari but a Ferrari-powered Haas. In 2016, sixteen-year-old New Zealander Marcus Armstrong joined the Ferrari Driver Academy, and by 2020 had progressed through Italian Formula Four to FIA Formula Two. Ferrari, and Mercedes-AMG,

The Academics: Red Bull Junior team member Jack Doohan with his father (top), five-time world motorcycle champion Mick, in 2021, contesting the FIA Formula 3 Championship. Doohan is up against several second- and third-generation racers—Enzo Fittipaldi, grandson of two-time world champion Emerson, and David Schumacher, son of Ralf and nephew of seven-time world champion Michael. New Zealander Marcus Armstrong (bottom), part of the Ferrari Driving Academy, is contesting the FIA Formula 2 Championship in 2021.

used their academies to provide drivers, as well as power plants, to their constructor customers. Mercedes-AMG had placed George Russell with Williams-Mercedes. Alpine F1—without an engine customer in 2021—was fostering Oscar Piastri with a view to moving him to their own F1 team.

In 2021, thanks to the academies, three drivers from Australia and New Zealand—Lawson, Armstrong and Piastri—were facing off against each other in Formula Two, on the springboard to a F1 career.

The academies (and Red Bull especially has developed a reputation) can be brutal. With such a wealth of talent eager to get in, the churn can afford to be great. In the mid-2000s, Australian Nathan Antunes, one year behind Vettel, lost his place with Red Bull without explanation. 'It's been very difficult to recover from that, a very traumatic time and to be honest we struggled,' his dad Cas told me. But to be provided with the opportunity is the call of a lifetime.

Shane Wharton had climbed a tree overlooking Ferrari's Fiorano test track in Maranello. Stopwatch in hand, he was timing a succession of spindly Formula Four cars through a section of track he'd roughed out. He had his eyes on one in particular. 'My word, maybe this young Australian is going to give everyone a hard time,' he chuckled to himself. It was day three into an eight-day selection program being run by the Ferrari Driver Academy. Parents had been banned from the track and Shane had gone clandestine.

'We got a text from Motorsport Australia asking us to apply for the Ferrari Driver Academy,' Shane Wharton said from his near-permanent home in Italy. By 'we', he meant his son James. The father-and-son team had spent two years on the road, living in Italy, kart racing, a discipline at which young James is highly proficient. 'I said no,' Shane said. 'He'd just turned fourteen—far too young. Besides, it had been nine months since James and I had been home.' Shane was keen to reunite with his wife Janette and twelve-year-old daughter Jacqueline in Melbourne. 'It's what you do for your kids,' he said.

James Wharton, here aged fourteen, is Australia's next long-range Formula One hope. In December 2020, Wharton received congratulations at Motorsport Australia's Melbourne headquarters from director of racing operations Tim Schenken, veteran of 34 grands prix starts. Motorsport Australia has renewed its efforts to identify fresh talent across the Oceania region.

COVID-19 had made 2020 a strange year. Motorsport Australia had been unable to conduct Ferrari's regional selection program in the prescribed manner. Instead, it took advice from organisations throughout Asia-Pacific about youngsters with talent and ambition. Two were chosen. The youngest, James Wharton, was geographically accessible. He and his dad were living at Bassano del Grappa in the Veneto, close by the Parolin Racing Kart factory for which James raced. They only had to drive 200 kilometres to the gates of Fiorano. 'I relented and said we'd go, just for the experience,' Shane said.

Ferrari's selection process was rigorous. It took into account intelligence, fitness, psychology, commercial acumen, media preparedness, education, technical

On the way to school. James Wharton proudly sent his dad Shane this picture on his first day at the Ferrari Driver Academy. He's in Ferrari uniform—including a Prancing Horse COVID-19 face mask—and he's walking down the runway at Ferrari's Fiorano test track next to the office once occupied by the Commendatore.

New Zealand's one-make Toyota Racing Series has become a counter-seasonal discovery championship for young hopefuls. It has been won by Lando Norris and Lance Stroll, both now entrenched in Formula One. In 2019 it was won by local driver Liam Lawson, shown here competing at Teretonga the following year. Lawson is now racing in the FIA Formula 2 Championship.

skills and mechanical sympathy, as well as driving ability and racecraft. At the conclusion of the program, Ferrari offered James a contract. It was for ten years and it mapped out a clear path all the way to F1.

His aim from the time he first drove a go-kart, aged seven, was to be on this rung of the ladder.

'I had budgeted $10 million,' Shane, who owns a steel-fabrication business in Melbourne, said. 'That was enough to get him to Formula Two. We'd planned to be there by the time he was nineteen.'

Ferrari hadn't totally relieved the financial pressure. Their investment in their academy members is shared with the families, but to what degree Shane is contractually unable to reveal. What would happen, I enquired, if your son woke up tomorrow and decided to play tennis instead? 'A penalty would apply,' he conceded. 'But that's not going to happen.'

Ferrari's commitment is full on. James is a residential student at Ferrari's Formula One boarding school in Maranello. He continues to do distance education with a high school in Victoria, covering the basic subjects until he at least reaches Year 10.

In 2021, he and his dad were apart for the first time in seven years of travelling the karting trail, but Shane remained in Italy. Each weekend he picked James up and took him to his scheduled kart races. 'I will never miss a lap of James on a track,' he said.

James planned to stay with karting until he turned fifteen and was able to enter the European Formula Four championship. His birthday is in the middle of the year, and the Whartons are too canny to enter him halfway through the season. 'He needs to have a big chance of winning Rookie of the Year, so he'll hold back until he can do the full season.'

James Wharton could well be typical of a new breed of Formula One aspirants: motivated at an early age by the quality media that covers F1, empowered by the opportunity now available at junior level, and enabled, if they're extremely fortunate, by parents like Shane, who are prepared to invest in their dreams. It's far removed in terms of cost but maybe not in commitment from the swimming parent on their pre-dawn drive to the training pool. For every hundred kids who pound their chilly laps, few will make it to the Olympics. As more kids leap into the F1 training pond, the same ratio may well apply.

'Four years ago, we went to Fiorano on a bus tour,' Shane said. 'James was ten and he didn't say much—just pressed his nose to the window. But as we were leaving, he said: "I'm thinking I'll be back here as a driver."'

Midway through 2021, Motorsport Australia renewed its contract with the Ferrari Driver Academy to continue its relentless search for our next world champion. Concurrently, in New Zealand, the Kiwi Driver Fund ramped up test days with its one-make FT60 Formula Three cars, inviting young hopefuls from Australia to participate as well. The two initiatives, side-by-side, provide hope that the region's 40-year world championship drought can be brought to an end.

THE HONOUR ROLL

AUSTRALIA

World championship contestants	Non-championship contestants	Tests
Jack Brabham 🏁	Bruce Allison	Ryan Briscoe
David Brabham	Keith Campbell	James Courtney
Gary Brabham	Ken Kavanagh	Will Davison
Warwick Brown	Brian McGuire	Oscar Piastri
Paul England	Stephen Ouvaroff	Will Power
Frank Gardner		
Tony Gaze		
Paul Hawkins		
Alan Jones 🏁		
Larry Perkins		
Daniel Ricciardo		
Tim Schenken		
Vern Schuppan		
David Walker		
Mark Webber		

VIP drivers
Mick Doohan
Wayne Gardner
Craig Lowndes
Mark Skaife

NEW ZEALAND

World championship contestants	Non-championship contestants	Tests
Chris Amon	Ronnie Moore	Scott Dixon
Howden Ganley	Ray Thackwell	
Brendon Hartley		
Denny Hulme 🏁		
Bruce McLaren		
Graham McRae		
John Nicholson		
Tony Shelly		
Mike Thackwell		

ABOUT THE AUTHOR

JOHN SMAILES is a journalist, motorsport commentator and publicist. He was the managing editor of the 60th-anniversary history of the Confederation of Australian Motor Sport, now Motorsport Australia, the governing body of Australian motor racing. For Allen & Unwin he has written *Climbing the Mountain,* the autobiography of Australian motorsport legend Allan Moffat OBE; *Race Across the World,* the incredible story of the 1968 London–Sydney Marathon and a sequel to *The Bright Eyes of Danger,* which he wrote with the first Australian Touring Car Champion David McKay; *Mount Panorama,* the full history of Australia's most revered motor racing circuit for cars and motorcycles; and *Speed Kings,* which chronicles the attempts by Australians and New Zealanders to conquer the greatest Super Speedway of all. *Formula One* has been driven by John's lifelong enthusiasm for the category that is at the pinnacle of all motor sport.

www.johnsmailes.com.au

At the 2000 Singapore GP, author John Smailes with Red Bull teammates Sebastian Vettel and Mark Webber.

ACKNOWLEDGEMENTS

JACK BRABHAM WAS THE FIRST RACING DRIVER I EVER
met. He was a 34-year-old double world Formula One champion (and went on to total three); I was a schoolboy attending my first motor race. Jack gave my dad and me all the time in the world and of course he won—a 100-mile (160-kilometre) race around Mount Panorama, Bathurst, which had been convened in his honour. The last time I met with Jack was at his home shortly before he died in 2014, when he set me straight on at least some of the misnomers that had attached themselves to his illustrious CV. It was as if he was correcting the record.

Since Jack first went to Europe in 1954, 23 Australians and New Zealanders—24 counting Tony Gaze who went before—have tried to scale the mountain that is world championship Formula One. Apart from Jack, two had each claimed a single world crown and another three had won grands prix. Incredibly, their achievements had never been chronicled, at least not in one book. I put the idea to Jack at our final meeting. His ambivalence was resounding. 'You're either quick or you're not' was his racing catch cry, and the same principle, it seemed, applied to the paddock in general. Still, the idea for this book was born that day and I acknowledge Jack's part in its genesis.

Jack is one of ten of the 24 who are no longer with us. Happily, I had met and interviewed the majority, so, with the help of top-ups from family, friends and historians, this book has been able to offer something more than a textbook perspective of their careers. Thanks, particularly, to Michael Clark and Brian Lawrence in New Zealand and Mark Bisset and Gerald McDornan in Australia. Of the others, to Ann and Mark Webber, sincere thanks for allowing me unfettered access to your published memoirs; to Aaron Noonan and Greg Siddle, for your insight into the reclusive Larry Perkins; and to Joe Ricciardo and Bryan Hartley, massive thanks for the parent's-eye view of your high-achieving sons.

Formula One is a high-tech village, motor racing's version of Silicon Valley. It's secretive and competitive, yet brimful of mutual respect. Sam Michael, one of Australia's must successful F1 exports, was generous in setting up contact with his peers—Australasian engineers and technologists who have contributed to the exponential growth of the category. Sam also read the first draft for fact.

Drivers and families gave freely of their photographic archives—the Brabham family's early shots of the boys with their dad are a prime example. Then, the incredibly helpful Stephen West made 26 million photographs available through Britain's fast-growing Motorsport Images library, a venture whose president is former F1 commentator James Allen. Selecting from its images was a joy, especially as it kept throwing up one-off gems: Australia's first touring car champion David McKay, bare chested (in the style of Stirling Moss) in the pits with Denny Hulme; doyen Australian journalist Mike Kable with Chris Amon at Monaco; Max Mosley with David Brabham on the day Ayrton Senna died, sparking Mosley's F1 safety crusade.

Allen & Unwin's publishing director Tom Gilliatt suggested *Formula One* as a sequel to *Speed Kings*, the story of Down Under exploits at the Indianapolis 500. He was more enthusiastic for the project than Jack Brabham, and rightly so. This is now the fifth in what has become a series of motor-racing books published by Allen & Unwin, and along with a happily growing number of readers, I'm grateful for their support in bringing motorsport to the masses.

Senior editor Samantha Kent is now working on her third motor-racing title and despite her best attempts to remain detached, she's becoming a confirmed rev-head. Sam leads a team of increasingly like-minded professionals—demon copy editor Emma Driver, proofreader Cassie Holland, designer Philip Campbell and typesetter Simon Paterson who put in an immense effort into what became 'our project'. Thank you to each of them.

Formula One brings to a conclusion decades of family dispute, and Jenny, Andrew, Kate, Karen, Dan, Cameron and Matilda are now satisfied that resolution has been reached on what constitutes a Formula One driver and how many actually exist from our region. The numbers have always been rubbery, but as of publication, fifteen Australians and nine New Zealanders have raced in a world championship race in the Formula One era, from 1950. Another thirteen, ten of them Australians, have tested a Formula One car or driven in a non-championship race. Young Oscar Piastri is one of the thirteen, and hopefully he will soon graduate to the active list.

BIBLIOGRAPHY

BOOKS

Boddy, W., *The History of Motor Racing,* London: Orbis Publishing, 1980

Brabham, J., Nye, D., *The Jack Brabham Story,* Windsor, NSW: Minidi Press, 2004

Clark, M., *Denny Hulme: A celebration of a Kiwi icon,* Auckland: Bruce McLaren Trust, 2012

Collerson, B., *Mount Druitt to Monza: Motor racing on a shoestring budget*, Sydney: Bookworks, 2004

Cox, D., *Circus Life: Australian motorcycle racers in Europe in the 1950s,* Sydney: Plimsoll Street Publishing, 2012

Davis, T., Armont, A., *Brabham: The untold story of Formula One,* Sydney: HarperCollins, 2019

Gardner, F., *Drive to Survive,* Sydney: Drive Publishing, 1984

Georgano, G.N., *The Encyclopaedia of Motor Sport,* London: Ebury Press, 1971

Henderson, M., *Motor Racing in Safety,* London: Patrick Stephens, 1968

Henry, A., *Williams: Triumph out of tragedy,* Sparkford, UK: Patrick Stephens, 1995

Hill, T., *Formula One: The complete story,* Croxley Green, UK: Transatlantic Press, 2009

Howard, G., *The Official 50-Race History of the Australian Grand Prix,* Australia: R&T Publishing, 1986

Jones, A., Botsford, K., *Alan Jones: Driving ambition,* London: Stanley Paul, 1981

Jones, A., Clarke, A., *AJ: How Alan Jones climbed to the top of Formula One,* Sydney: Penguin Random House, 2017

Kerr, P., *To Finish First,* Auckland: Random House NZ, 2007

Lawrence, M., *The Ron Tauranac Story,* London: Brooklands Books, 1999

Martin, S., *Historic Ferrari and Grand Prix Cars: My Life,* Australia: Spencer Martin, 2020

McKay, D., *David McKay's Scuderia Veloce,* Sydney: Turton & Armstrong, 2001

McLeod, I., *'Hawkeye',* London: MRP Publishing, 2003

Moore, A., *Aintree Down Under: Warwick Farm and the golden age of Australian motor sport,* Sydney: Walla Walla Press, 2017

Neubauer, A., *Speed was My Life,* London: Barrie & Rockcliff, 1960

Nye, D., *The Classic Single-Seaters,* London: Macmillan Leisure Books, 1975

Nye, D., *McLaren: The grand prix, CAN-AM and Indy Cars,* Richmond, UK: Hazleton Publishing, 1984

Owen, A., *The Racing Coopers,* London: Cassell & Company, 1960

Price, D., *Joan Richmond: From Melbourne to Monte Carlo and beyond,* Melbourne: JR Publishing, 2011

Saunders, N., *Daniel Ricciardo: In pursuit of greatness,* Melbourne: Hardie Grant Books, 2018

Saward, J., *The World Atlas of Motor Racing,* London: Hamlyn Publishing Group, 1989

Shepherd, J., *A History of Australian Speedway,* Sydney: Frew Publications, 2003

Small, S., *Grand Prix Who's Who* (3rd ed.), Reading, UK: Travel Publishing Limited, 2000

Webber, M., *Aussie Grit,* Sydney: Pan Macmillan, 2015

Wilson, S., *Almost Unknown: Squadron Leader Tony Gaze OAM,* Sydney: Chevron Publishing Group, 2009

Woods, B., *Legends of Speed,* Sydney: HarperCollins, 2004

Young, E., *Forza Amon! A biography of Chris Amon,* Auckland: HarperSports, 2003

INTERVIEWS

Allison, Bruce: Brisbane, March 2021
Antunes, Cas: Sydney, February 2021
Bernasconi, Paul: Sydney, March 2021
Brabham, David: London, January 2021
Brabham, Gary: Queensland, February 2021
Brabham, Geoffrey: Indianapolis, USA, March 2021
Briscoe, Ryan: Connecticut, USA, February 2020
Brown, Bill (on Paul Hawkins): Sydney, March 2021
Brown, Warwick: Sydney, March 2021
Clark, Michael (on Tony Shelly and John Nicholson): New Zealand, April 2021
Connelly, Garry: Brisbane, March 2021
Courtney, James: Melbourne, March 2021
Davison, Will: Gold Coast, Qld, February 2021
Dixon, Scott: Indianapolis, USA, February 2020
Dyer, Chris: UK, February 2021
Ganley, Howden: California, USA, February 2021
Gardner, Gloria: Gold Coast, Qld, February 2021
Hartley, Bryan: New Zealand, February 2021
Henderson, Michael: Sydney, June 2021
Hobbs, David (on Frank Gardner and Paul Hawkins): Miami, USA, March 2021
Hulme, Greeta; Rotorua, New Zealand, December 2019
Jones, Alan: Gold Coast, Qld, April 2021
Masi, Michael: Sydney, January 2021
McLaren, Jan (on Bruce McLaren): New Zealand, December 2019
McRae, Graham: New Zealand, December 2019
Michael, Sam: Sydney, January 2021
Noonan, Aaron (podcast on Larry Perkins): Melbourne, March 2021
Oastler, Malcolm: South Coast NSW, March 2021
Piastri, Chris, Nicole and Oscar: Melbourne, January 2021
Power, Will: North Carolina, USA, February 2020
Ricciardo, Joe: Perth, February 2021
Roby, Steve: North Carolina, USA, January 2021
Schenken, Tim: Melbourne, January 2021
Schuppan, Vern: Adelaide, March 2021
Sharizman, Mia: UK, February 2021
Siddle, Greg: Sydney, February 2021
Smith, Michael: Melbourne, April 2021
Tauranac, Ron: Sunshine Coast, Qld, February 2020
Thackwell, Ray (on Mike Thackwell): Perth, March 2021
Toet, Willem: Switzerland, February 2021
Walker, David: Mandalay, Qld, January 2021
Webber, Mark and Ann (access to memoirs): Noosa, Qld, April 2021
Wharton, Shane: Italy, March 2021
Windsor, Peter: UK, February 2021

INDEX

Page numbers in *italics* refer to image captions.

PICTORIAL ATTRIBUTION

Allison family: p. 223; Alpine Racing: pp. x, 2–3, 4, 10; Australian National Museum: pp. 16, 28, 31; Brabham family: pp. 66, 70, 72; Bruce McLaren Trust: p. 108; Chevron Publishing: pp. 20, 83, 158, 268; Davison family: pp. 34, 36; England family: p. 210; Michael Henderson: p. 265; Mark Horsburgh/Scott Wensley: pp. 232, 234; Indianapolis Motor Speedway: pp. 74 (top), 111; Motorsport Australia: p. 276; Jonathan Panoff (www.jonathanpanoff.com.au): p. 241; Nathan Johnston: p. 281; Piastri family: p. 12; Tim Schenken: p. 138; Max Stahl: p. 91; John Smailes: p. 59; Simon Sostaric: p. 14; The Project Group: p. 255; Toyota New Zealand/Bruce Jenkins Photography: p. 278; David Walker: p. 125; Wharton family: p. 277; unattributable: pp. 25, 38, 268.

All other photographs: Motorsport Images

Front cover: Daniel Ricciardo sensationally debuted the Red Bull Racing RB10 at the 2014 Australian F1 Grand Prix, qualified second, finished second and became the first Australian to take a podium finish in his home world championship—only to be disqualified for a technical rule infringement.

Pages iv–v: Two new cars for the 2021 season. Daniel Ricciardo (McLaren MCL35M) leads four-time world champion Sebastian Vettel (Aston Martin AMR21) on the Algarve International Circuit in Portugal.

Back cover: A chequerboard of champions, each a podium place-getter.
From top left to bottom right: Tim Schenken, Bruce McLaren, Daniel Ricciardo, Denny Hulme, Mark Webber, Alan Jones, Chris Amon, Jack Brabham.

Allen & Unwin
83 Alexander Street
Crows Nest NSW 2065
Australia
Phone: (61 2) 8425 0100
Email: info@allenandunwin.com
Web: www.allenandunwin.com

A catalogue record for this book is available from the National Library of Australia

ISBN 978 1 76106 531 6

Internal design by Philip Campbell Design
Set in 11/15 pt Callum by Bookhouse
Printed and bound in China by C&C Offset Printing Co. Ltd

10 9 8 7 6 5 4 3 2 1